MICHAELS DESSERTS

Sweets for a Cause

MICHAEL C. PLATT

GET CREATIVE 6

Get Greative 6
An imprint of Mixed Media Resources
19 West 21st Street, Suit 601
New York, NY 10010
sixthandspringbooks.com

Editors TODD HUNTER, PAMELA WISSMAN

Creative Director IRENE LEDWITH

Designer STACY WAKEFIELD FORTE

Cover photo by FARRAH SKEIKY

Recipe photos by FARRAH SKEIKY and KRISTEN WILKES

Chief Executive Officer CAROLINE KILMER

President ART JOINNIDES

Chairman JAY STEIN

DEDICATION
I dedicate this book to the kids who are working to change the world. No matter how big or small, your work is important. Do everything you can and never give up.

Always follow safety and commonsense cooking protocol while using kitchen utensils, operating ovens and stoves, and handling uncooked food. If children are participating in the preparation of any recipe, they should always be supervised by an adult.

Library of Congress Cataloging-in-Publication Data available upon request.

Printed in China

1 3 5 7 9 10 8 6 4 2

First Edition

ACKNOWLEDGMENTS

I'd like to acknowledge the people who inspired these recipes and my love for food and baking. To my family, for whom food has played a huge part. There is so much history in a lot of these recipes and I wouldn't be able to share them as authentically as I am without the connection to them. To my mom, who taught me a lot about baking and helped me test and develop these recipes. I wouldn't have the skill set or opportunity to write this book without her. Thank you for helping me develop and understand my love for food. To my dad, thank you for being supportive, encouraging me, and always believing in what I'm doing. To my brother Gabriel, thank you for being very supportive throughout the process, helping out in every way you can, and taste-testing my creations, even the questionable ones, over the years.

I'd also like to mention the team who helped create the book. To Mrs. Pamela, thank you for giving me this opportunity and the direction I needed to write this book. To Mrs. Irene, thank you for the creative direction and for helping bring my vision for this book to life. To Todd Hunter and Mocha Ochoa, because who knows where we'd be without you guys. And to Farrah, thank you for the beautiful photos; these recipes have never looked better!

ABOUT THE AUTHOR

MICHAEL C. PLATT is a baker, social entrepreneur, and food justice advocate. He is the founder PLLATE, an initiative that creates snack packs for kids experiencing food insecurity, and Michaels Desserts which uses a 1-for-1 model to donate a dessert to someone in need for every one that is sold. Michael has served hundreds of people through his initiatives.

Raised in a home of educators and advocates, Michael started baking at nine years old and has been committed to the challenges of inequality since learning about the March on Washington at age six. When he is not baking, Michael enjoys experimenting with film photography and digital art design, riding his longboard, and spending time with his family and friends. He lives in the Washington DC area with his parents, older brother Gabriel, his two dogs Cornbread and Biscuit, and two cats Blueberry and Isis. To learn more about Michael, visit www.michaelsdesserts.com.

CONTENTS

NO KID HUNGRY FRENCH TOAST CUPCAKES

OREO CAKE! ----->

3 Cakes

4 Snacks & Breads

SWEET POTATO PIE

Teaching a cupcake decorating class at Williams Sonoma to raise money for NKH , 2019.

INTRODUCTION

*H*ello, my name is Michael Platt. I'm a sixteen-year-old entrepreneur. And I love baking and cooking.

My love affair with food started at home. Spending time with loved ones in the kitchen, with those sweet and savory smells filling the house . . . it's so special. My family is passionate about cooking. At our family dinners, everyone makes their specialty dish and many of the recipes have a story behind them. The stories are either about the origin of a recipe or how it was passed down through the generations. Sharing stories and sharing food just makes you feel good.

With so much love for food around me, I soon fell in love with baking. The first dish I ever baked was a layered chocolate cake, the kind that comes in a box. I was nine years old. My grandma Sarah helped me, but she let me take the lead. Since I made that first cake I have never looked back. My favorite part about baking is the finishing touches. I am amazed every time I see how the icing and decorations come together, turning a cupcake into a piece of art. And then it's also about the feeling of accomplishment. You have something that starts with eggs, flour, sugar, and other ingredients and it ends up being a delicious baked treat. It's basically chemistry and I love science. Baking is really just the cooking version of science.

Invited by Susan Axelrod and Beth Dean of CURE Epilepsy, an organization that funds research to find a cure for epilepsy, Michael shares his story with David Axelrod at their 2019 fundraiser in Chicago.

Michael with the owners of Eli's Cheesecake, Marc Schulman and his daughter Elana Schulman with Beth Dean (on right), the CEO of CURE Epilepsy. At Eli's, Michael developed his CURE cupcake recipe and later donated sweet treats to a local shelter in Chicago.

Although my grandmother introduced me to baking, it was something else entirely that took my baking to the next level.

In fourth grade, I began to experience disruption in my vision and doctors thought it was caused by migraines. Doctors searched for a while trying to figure out why this was happening. We didn't find out until the summer before sixth grade, when I had a grand mal seizure after coming back home from summer camp. The disruptions in my vision were actually auras. These are small seizures warning me that a bigger seizure might be on the way. It's kind of like when you feel a few droplets of rain before the storm arrives. The auras didn't happen all the time, but they could be triggered if I let myself become dehydrated or fatigued.

The doctors diagnosed me with epilepsy. I would soon learn that epilepsy was a neurological disease. It is a "misfire" in the brain that can happen in one part of the brain or throughout the entire brain. This misfiring meant that my brain wasn't communicating the correct information to my body. Sometimes I would experience short-term memory loss as a result of all the abnormal brain activity.

I was cautioned by doctors to reduce my physical activity so the seizures could be controlled by medication. All of a sudden I had to stop doing things I loved to do, like gymnastics, swimming, climbing trees, and riding my bike. I needed to find something else to occupy my time and attention. I needed a creative outlet. This is when I leaned into baking even more. It was one thing I enjoyed that didn't have any restrictions. Now, I had more time to bake all kinds of things—cakes, cupcakes, brownies, cookies, muffins. Are you drooling yet? The added benefit of baking is having to remember all the steps and techniques, which helped me learn to manage some of my memory loss.

"I've seen a cupcake inspire smiles, tears, amazement, joy, satisfaction, happiness, and other private emotions that I won't share out of respect for people's dignity."

MICHAELS DESSERTS

I was ten years old when my parents bought me a pair of TOMS shoes as a Christmas present. They knew I liked TOMS shoes, but as a family, we also enjoyed how the brand gave back. Inside the shoebox was a card that explained the company's business model: for every pair of shoes purchased, the company would give a pair of new shoes to a child who needed them. My parents didn't know it, but I had decided that I wanted to start a business. When I learned how TOMS operated, I decided that was the way I wanted to run mine.

The charitable part of TOMS was impressive to me because I didn't hear about a lot of businesses that donated their product for a good cause. From my family I learned the value of giving back and thought a business would be a great way to do that—equity and justice were always important to me. When I was younger, I remember hearing stories about the work of the civil rights leaders who fought for freedom and justice. I would ask my grandparents questions about the movement and the reasons behind it. We

had so many conversations . . . and still do. There were some, like Martin Luther King Jr. and Harriet Tubman, who made great sacrifices for what they believed in. Talk about giving back. I was so inspired by some of these individuals that I made cupcakes to honor them. The Dr. King and Booker T. Washington cupcakes are fan favorites. On top of that, I've seen my parents, grandparents, aunts, and uncles organize or volunteer for numerous community-focused grassroots organizations. They are my role models.

When I was thinking about starting a business, I wanted to follow the tradition of those who sacrifice for others and the examples I had in my family. My parents helped me hone in on a cause that I truly care about: food insecurity. I have always believed that everyone should have access to basic necessities like food, regardless of their income or status in life. I knew there were families who didn't regularly eat three meals a day the way other families did because they lacked money to buy food. I saw kids, some of whom were my classmates, who depended on breakfast and lunch at school, and who were unsure whether there would be enough for dinner at home. During a school break—summer or a holiday, for instance—they were even less likely to get three meals. On top of all that, you have whole communities that don't have access to a grocery store where they can buy nutritional food for their families.

> "I've passed a cupcake to someone sitting with all their possessions in a shopping cart and had them tell me that this one simple act gave them hope. I've left a cupcake beside someone who's sleeping under blankets on a grate because their friend on the grate next to them said it was OK when I asked. That's why I give away cupcakes."

Michael with Jordan Carfagno, principal culinary training and development manager at McCormick & Company. McCormick invited him to "play" in their state-of-the-art kitchens with their chefs. That is how Michael finished developing No Kid Hungry French Toast Cupcakes (page 34) and Nelson Mandela Malva Pudding Cupcakes (page 46).

A year after I received those TOMS shoes, I decided to fuse my passion for baking with helping to alleviate food insecurity and Michaels Desserts was born. Michaels Desserts was my way to help feed kids and adults who may not get to enjoy a sweet treat. When parents fall on hard times, the extra things that used to happen regularly, like going to the movies or making homemade desserts, sometimes stop. With my baked goods, I could give people something memorable to brighten their day and feed those who might be having a difficult time.

Michaels Desserts follows a business model similar to TOMS. When we receive enough orders to make a batch of cupcakes, we match the ordered amount to donate to local shelters. Then we pack up the cupcakes and drop them off the same day or early the next day. We want to make sure that the shelters are receiving fresh tasty treats.

Sometimes I am asked why there is no apostrophe in the first word—Michaels— of the business name. Well, there's a simple answer for that: In grammar, apostrophes represent possession or ownership. When I created Michaels Desserts, I am reminded that I am not doing this for myself, but for other people.

POWER, LOVE, LEARNING, AND ACCESS TO EVERYONE

Michaels Desserts is doing its part to alleviate food insecurity, but I wanted to do even more. Two years after founding Michaels Desserts, at the age of thirteen, I started a nonprofit called PLLATE, which stands for Power, Love, Learning, and Access To Everyone.

PLLATE is an initiative where we create snack packs for kids who may be experiencing food insecurity. The snack packs are small bags of healthy, protein-forward, nonperishable foods such as granola bars, nuts, dried fruit, and beef jerky. We know that a lot of kids might eat breakfast but not eat lunch and/or may not know whether they will eat dinner. So the snack packs can be eaten when needed—when a child is hungry, waiting for his or her next meal.

Let me break down PLLATE even further:

POWER–Giving people the power to be able to feed themselves. This means not just giving people food, but giving people the knowledge to be able to grow their own food, cook the food they have, or access the food that will sustain them.

LOVE–I want people to feel loved when they interact with PLATTE. Like

someone cares about them enough to help with their basic needs.

LEARNING–Everyone learns. I want to teach people without access to food how to get it and the people with access to food how they can help others.

ATE–Access to everyone. Food should be accessible to everyone who needs it.

PLLATE donates to local food pantries and organizations that work closely with the community. Our goal is for snack packs to reach those who need them most. I was proud that we were able to extend PLLATE to after-school programs that were then able to distribute to families and children in need. This had always been a goal of mine.

Between Michaels Desserts and PLLATE, we have donated more than 500,000 meals. Before the COVID-19 pandemic, the number of children possibly facing food insecurity moved from one in six to one in seven, as reported by Feeding America, a nationwide network of food banks. I was very proud of that progress because it meant that the collective effort by those of us working to eradicate food insecurity was moving the needle. There have been some setbacks since then because of the COVID-19 pandemic. It's understandable because none of us could foresee how the pandemic would affect people accessing food. But as we turn the corner on COVID-19, I am confident that we will have even greater success in lowering the number of those who face food insecurity every day.

MICHAEL STRAHAN

Left: The two Michaels on the set of *Good Morning America*, New York City, 2019, where Michael was acknowledged for his baking and work toward ending food insecurity.

Below: Michael with members of the *Good Morning Washington* team after demonstrating how to make Spicy Hot Chocolate Cupcakes and Golden Milk Cupcakes, Christmas, 2021.

Kids Can Help Solve
BIG PROBLEMS!

I also want to share a message I believe with all my heart, and one that I shared in my TEDx talk a couple of years ago. Small people can help solve big problems! One group that I think can make the biggest change is kids. People often underestimate the power of kids. They certainly underestimate our power to do something about big problems, but I think we can do a lot. The world would be an even better place if kids were involved in helping to solve important issues, especially because we're usually the ones being affected by them the most. Take gun control laws in relatioship to school safety, for example. It's the kids who are having these horrible experiences and we should have a say in how these problems are solved because we're the ones who are being affected by it.

CHEF SPIKE MENDELSOHN

Michael with Chef Spike Mendelsohn at a 2019 event for Food Rescue DC, an organization that helps transport food from restaurants that would be thrown away to organizations that can use the food to feed people.

Unfortunately, some adults think that kids don't have anything meaningful to contribute. One of my favorite quotes is 1 Timothy, chapter 4, verse 12: "Don't let anyone look down on you because you are young, but set an example for the believers in speech, in life, in love, in faith, and in purity." When I first heard this, I instantly loved it because I think this amazing world needs kids to lead with our speech, lives, love, faith, and purity.

No matter how you look at it, there are important issues that humanity regularly struggles with—hunger, gun violence, racism, school safety, and more—and all of these are issues that deeply impact kids. I believe kids can choose a problem they are passionate about and help solve it. I chose hunger as the problem that I would help solve. Hunger is a serious issue that impacts a significant amount of families worldwide. This can create a loop of poverty for families, and that affects kids. Hunger can lead to a lack of focus, which can lead to poor grades, lack of education, and problems getting a good job later, and all of that can lead to experiencing a cycle of poverty. The cycle then repeats again, starting and ending with kids. In any normal-size classroom in America it's possible for five kids to be unsure of where their next meal is going to come from. Worldwide, hunger kills more people than malaria, tuberculosis, and AIDS combined. In the United States, 45 million people, 20 million of them being kids, rely on SNAP (Supplemental Nutrition Assistance Program) benefits to buy enough food each month.

For my entire life, my family has been involved in the community. My grandfather was a Boy Scout troop leader,

What's Next For
MICHAELS DESSERTS & PLLATE

What can you do to help the most people with food insecurity? This is the question I ask myself regularly. This is the question that drives Michaels Desserts and PLLATE.

I believe that an even wider network is needed to address hunger in our communities—and kids can be fully involved if given the support. My big vision for Michaels Desserts and PLLATE includes incorporating people from the community to join the mission and collaborating with No Kid Hungry, which I have been an ambassador for since 2017, and other organizations that serve individuals facing food insecurity.

As Michaels Desserts and PLLATE continue to grow, I would love to expand the business into these other areas that address food insecurity in our communities:

YOUTH AWARENESS: I want to encourage you to do the same work I do. And it doesn't take much to get involved. It starts with conversations at home. Adults can talk to the young people in their lives about the value of giving and how to incorporate it into their lives.

SHARED KITCHEN: Cooking by design gives people access to food, even if they can't afford it. I foresee owning a shared kitchen for people who want to start a cooking business and who need access to a commercial kitchen. They would be encouraged to give back to the community as part of their business.

BUDGET COOKING CLASSES: The purpose of the cooking classes is to teach people how to cook one-pot, shelf-stable meals that can last for several days and how to make bread from scratch, as well as other items that are easy to make. These are meals that don't use many ingredients but from which several meal items can be made.

SMALL SPACE GARDENING CLASSES: I created my first small space gardening kit last year: soil, seed, and a small LED light that can be used to help plant growth in spaces that may not be well lit. It's especially helpful to grow seasonings that can give often-eaten food different flavors so that families in need can enjoy tasty foods. There is a ton of possibilities that can come from these classes, especially if I can get them into the schools.

PAY-WHAT-YOU-CAN GROCERY STORE: One day, I would like to open a pay-what-you-can grocery store that would allow people to buy food even if they don't have much to spend and allow families who have more to spend to pay more for their groceries to offset the expense of those with fewer funds. The point is for the store to be sustained by the community.

Above: Chocolatier Jacques Torres at *Good Morning America* in 2019. Michael was invited to spend the afternoon with Chef Torres learning all about chocolate. Right: Jerome Grant, executive chef of Sweet Home Cafe, with Michael at the National Museum of African American History and Culture.

and my mother gave homemade cups of soup and biscuits to those experiencing homelessness in the parks in D.C. These people are my role models along with others such as Dr. Martin Luther King Jr. and the other freedom fighters in this book. I have taught classes at Williams Sonoma, I've been on *Kids Baking Championship* on Food Network, and I've been on national news outlets like CNN, *Good Morning America*, the *Washington Post*, and many more, all in an effort to shine light on the issue of hunger.

Every kid can do something about the problem they want to solve. Take the issue that matters to you, get the support of adults in your life, and remember that

you can help solve big problems! Use your speech, life, love, faith, and purity.

And to you adults: Know that it's up to you to educate kids on how to solve big problems. I immediately knew I wanted to help with hunger, so I learned about its impact nationally and internationally and asked for support from the adults in my life. Kids also need help with overcoming discouragement because it will happen. People who don't see the solution can be very discouraging. I've been told, "Your business model isn't sustainable. You shouldn't be focused on ending hunger because the problem is too big and you're too young." I've also been told it's the wrong problem for me to be addressing.

MICHAEL'S MOM!

LIVE ON GMA

GMA CHRISTMAS 25 COUNTDOWN

TEEN ON A MISSION
15-YEAR-OLD HELPING KIDS WHO ARE FOOD INSECURE

abc
GOOD MORNING AMERICA.COM

Michael with his mother live on *Good Morning America*, 2020. The show invited Michael to share his story of creating the 12 Tuesdays of Giving initiative as a Spark Leader for the GivingTuesdaySpark organization. *GMA* shared his story and surprised him when McCormick donated $50,000 to the Maryland food bank in Michael's name.

I don't get discouraged though, because I have supportive adults in my life and I know how impactful my business model is. Even when people have fallen on hard times, their eyes light up when I hand them a cupcake. People smile, talk to me, and ask me if they can get some for their friends because they know someone was thinking about them. I would like all kids to know that they don't need to give in to discouragement when taking on a big problem. Choose a solution you believe in and don't let anything stop you.

Kids are a force! With support from adults, we can change the world. The truth is that we need to do everything we can if we want to see the kind of change that's needed. Kids, get out there. Give, educate, and get your friends involved with an issue that matters to you. And adults, listen respectfully to the kids and grandkids in your life. Why? Because people who are small really can help solve big problems!

I have big dreams, as you can tell, and I have always believed that anything is possible—even equity where it has been lacking. My advice to everyone, especially young people, is to do what you can. If you can give a lot, then do that. If it's just a little, that's OK, just do it. When it comes to food insecurity, it's likely that you know a schoolmate or community member who is experiencing it even if they don't know what to call it. It can be as simple as sharing your food with someone else and impacting that one person's life. Just know this: Hunger is a problem we know how to solve! Feed the people. Together we can make food insecurity a thing of the past.

GETTING STARTED

This book is for kids who are old enough to use a stove, knives, and a stand mixer independently, but be sure to get help from an adult if you need it. And for best results, here are a few tips to remember as you get started:

- Read the recipe before beginning.
- Have ingredients and tools ready to go.
- Wash your hands before you start.
- Wash all fruits and vegetables.
- Use oven mitts or pot holders.
- Remember that cooking and baking improve with practice, so be patient with yourself!

SPECIAL TOOLS YOU MAY NEED

Most kitchens already have essential tools like measuring cups and spoons, mixing spoons, spatulas, pastry and basting brushes, whisks, rolling pins, kitchen knives, baking pans, muffin pans, baking sheets, and other basics. You'll want to have these on hand for sure, but there are also some tools in this book that everyone may not have or be familiar with. You can substitute other tools, but these additional supplies will make the recipes easier. You can find them at specialty grocery stores, craft-supply stores, and kitchenware departments in larger stores that carry baking supplies. Some may be found in your regular supermarket (but not all).

MUFFIN TINS

SIFTER

PIPING BAG WITH TIPS

These are used to decorate or fill desserts. A piping bag is cone-shaped, with a small opening on one end to attach different tips (I mostly use a 1M star and open star tips). The large end is for filling the bag with frosting, filling, whipped cream, etc. There are several different types of piping bags (reusable, disposable, made of different materials). Make sure you know how to properly attach your tips with the kind of bag you're using.

To fill your piping bag, turn down the top half of the bag, then hold it under the fold to spoon in your frosting or filling. Don't fill it more than half full, then twist the top tightly just above where the frosting ends. Hold the bag in your dominant hand while holding the twist with your forefinger and thumb—you'll use this hand to squeeze the frosting out through the tip. Use the fingers of your other hand to guide the tip as you're squeezing out your frosting or filling. You may want to practice before trying it on finished desserts, but it's a fun technique to learn!

SIFTER

This is used to separate and break up clumps in dry ingredients such as flour, and sometimes used to combined ingredients. There are different types of sifters, but they all serve the same purpose. You can also use a fine-mesh sieve, or if you don't have any of these tools, you can make the recipe without sifting.

PIPING BAG + TIPS!

MIXER WITH ATTACHMENTS

I use a stand mixer or hand mixer with whisk, paddle, and dough hook attachments for these recipes. Just know that if a recipe calls for a stand mixer, you can use a hand mixer instead. Hand mixers are light, easy to store, and portable (you can mix anywhere, with your own bowls and pots). Stand mixers are faster and more powerful. You can also walk away from them and multitask while they do their work. They come with many attachments, but they're more expensive, they're heavy, and you need space to store them.

CUPCAKE CORER

CUPCAKE CORER

This is a tool that creates a perfect hole in the center of a baked cupcake for filling with icing or other edible fillings. Cupcake corers come in different types, but they pretty much work like little cookie cutters that go partway down into the cupcake to hollow out the center while leaving enough cupcake on the bottom and sides to hold together nicely. You can use a knife or spoon for this, but a cupcake corer makes it easier and neater.

12-CAVITY MINI TART PAN

This comes in handy for making multiple mini tarts, rather than needing to have a lot of individual pans on hand. It's convenient for making 2½" round tarts with your own favorite fillings!

HAND MIXER

STANDARD 9" PIE PAN

Most pie recipes call for a 9" pie pan, so you may already have one or more of these in your kitchen. Whether you're baking your first pie or are an experienced baker, having a pie pan on hand is a must. They come in a wide variety of materials and prices, from low-cost disposable pans to more expensive options.

STANDARD 9" TART PAN

There are many sizes of tart pans, but a 9" tart pan that is 1" high is good to start with (if it's a little bigger or smaller by 1" or so, that's OK). Tart pans also come in a variety of materials, some with removable bottoms to remove the rim before sliding the tart off the disk base and onto a serving plate.

9" TART PAN ---->

--- HIGH-SIDED BAKING PAN

HIGH-SIDED BAKING PANS

Rectangular and square high-sided baking pans are deeper than baking sheets, so they can hold runny batters and sauces, and are also better for things that need to be stirred once in a while.

MANDOLINE

This tool is for cutting vegetables and fruit into even, and often very thin, slices. Mandolines come in different styles, but they all have a blade and a smooth "runway" for sliding fruit back and forth across the blade. Most have a way to adjust the thickness of the slices, as well as a hand guard that holds the food in place and protects your hands. It's important that the blade is sharp enough to cut through your fruit easily. It's also important to be careful around that blade, and store it safely when not in use.

TWO 6" ROUND CAKE PANS

I usually use two smaller 6" wide x 2" high round cake pans for my cakes, then slice them into even, thinner layers after that. If you need to substitute different size pans, such as 8" or 9" cake pans, be wary of the baking time, because the dimensions of the cakes will change, so always keep your eye on the oven and begin checking for doneness earlier than the recipe states.

6" CAKE PANS

PARCHMENT PAPER

PARCHMENT PAPER

Many of my recipes call for parchment paper, which is a heat-resistant, nonstick paper used in baking. Lining your baking pans with parchment paper prevents sticking and browning. It also makes cleanup easier, because you don't have to scrub off as much gunk. It's also a good surface for rolling out dough. It makes things easier, but isn't an absolute necessity. If you don't have it, make sure you do a good job of greasing your pan with cooking spray, butter, or oil. You can also try using silicone baking mats.

OFFSET SPATULA

This is a long, narrow spatula with a thin, flat, blunt metal blade for spreading frosting onto a cake. You can use a table knife or butter knife if you don't have one, but an offset spatula makes things easier.

KITCHEN THERMOMETER

KITCHEN THERMOMETER

If you cook or bake regularly, you should invest in a good food thermometer to take the guesswork out of cooking. Kitchen thermometers come in different styles. Some are more simple, while others are more fancy.

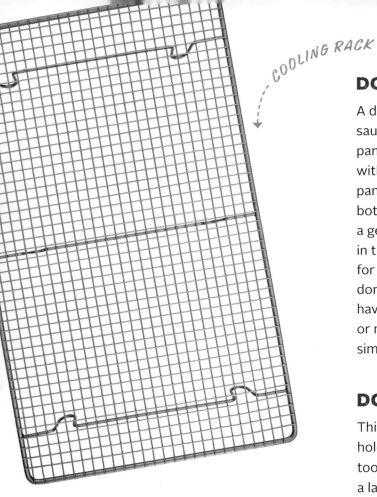

COOLING RACK

DOUBLE BOILER

A double boiler is just two pots: a large saucepan with a smaller, more shallow pan on top of it. You fill the bottom pan with 1" to 2" of water and set the shallow pan on top. Over heat, the water in the bottom pan begins to simmer, transferring a gentle heat to whatever you're cooking in the pan above. A double boiler is used for cooking delicate ingredients that don't do well over direct heat. If you don't have one, you can set a tempered glass or metal mixing bowl over a saucepan of simmering water.

DONUT CUTTER

This is like a cookie cutter that also cuts a hole in the middle for donuts. It's a great tool, but if you don't have one, you can use a large circle cookie cutter, then a smaller one for the hole. However, it's important to make sure the hole is large enough for donuts. If it's too small, it will fill in when the dough hits the fryer or is baked.

COOLING RACK

Many recipes will ask you to put freshly baked goods on a wire cooling rack. Wire racks allow air to circulate completely around whatever is on them, for faster cooling than if left on another surface. Wire cooling racks provide the best way to allow baked goods to cool more quickly and efficiently while preventing them from continuing to bake after you take them out of the oven.

DONUT CUTTER

6-OUNCE RAMEKINS

My Coffee Crème Brûlée (page 116) calls for eight 6-ounce ramekins. These are small round baking dishes that are surprisingly versatile for individually portioned desserts, including pies and snacks.

RAMEKINS

PAPER MUFFIN CUPS

JUMBO MUFFIN PAN

Make a bold statement with jumbo-size muffins or cupcakes! Each cup in a jumbo muffin pan holds more batter than traditional muffin cups, typically with a 3½" wide cup.

JUMBO PAPER MUFFIN CUPS

Jumbo muffin and cupcake liners are an easy way to make extra-large muffins and cupcakes. They can also be used for holding snacks and nuts, and come in different colors to match any occasion.

MALALA YOUSAFZAI
CARROT HALWA CUPCAKE!

1

Freedom Fighter Cupcakes

Cupcakes are one of my favorite things to bake. You can get very creative with them. These Freedom Fighter Cupcakes are inspired by people who motivate me to give back and support my community. The flavors are inspired by different things about the people, from where they come from, to their favorite desserts, or even their nicknames.

OVEN-TOASTED MARSHMALLOWS

Lay your marshmallows on a baking sheet (it helps to put parchment paper or aluminum foil down beforehand to make cleanup easier later), and set your oven to broil. Broil the marshmallows about 4" from the broiler until the tops are toasted golden brown, about 30 seconds to 1 minute. Keep a close eye on them to be sure they don't burn (you can even leave the oven door cracked a bit to do this).

Dr. Martin Luther King Jr.
SWEET POTATO PIE CUPCAKES

TIME: 45 MINUTES
MAKES: 18 CUPCAKES

SWEET POTATO PIE FILLING

- 2 well-roasted sweet potatoes (see page 51)
- 3 tbsp salted butter
- 3 tbsp heavy cream
- ⅓ cup brown sugar
- 1 tsp vanilla extract
- ½ tsp ground cinnamon
- ¼ tsp ground allspice
  Pinch of ground nutmeg

SPICED CUPCAKES

- 3 cups all-purpose flour
- 1½ tbsp baking powder
- ¾ tsp salt
- 2 tsp ground cinnamon
- 1 tsp ground allspice
- ½ tsp ground nutmeg
- 1 cup butter, at room temperature
- 2 cups granulated sugar
- 4 eggs
- 1 cup milk
- 1 tsp vanilla extract

ICING

- 8 ounces cold cream cheese
- 1⅓ cups powdered sugar
- 1 tsp ground cinnamon
- ½ tsp ground allspice
- ½ tsp ground nutmeg
- 2 cups cold heavy cream
- 1 tsp vanilla extract

GARNISH

- 54 toasted mini marshmallows or 18 standard-size toasted marshmallows

1 Preheat oven to 350°F.

2 For the cupcake filling, scoop roasted sweet potatoes from their skins into a medium bowl. Add butter, cream, brown sugar, vanilla, and spices. Mash and mix until incorporated. Set aside.

3 For the cupcakes, in a bowl, sift together flour, baking powder, salt, and spices. Set aside. With a stand mixer or hand mixer, cream butter until fluffy. Add granulated sugar. Continue to cream for 8 minutes. Add eggs one at a time, making sure they're incorporated but not overly mixed. Add one-third flour mix until incorporated. Combine milk and vanilla. Add half milk mixture (½ cup). Mix until combined. Alternate flour mix and milk, beginning and ending with flour, being careful not to overmix the batter. Gently fold in 1 cup of the sweet potato pie filling. Add the rest of the pie filling to a piping bag. Set aside. Line cupcake pans with 18 liners. Divide batter among liners and bake for 15 minutes until a toothpick inserted in the middle comes out clean. Set cupcakes aside to cool.

4 Carefully core out middle of each cupcake with a cupcake corer or knife. Fill each with filling using a piping bag.

5 For the icing, in a bowl, whip cream cheese with a whisk attachment on medium speed until smooth. Add powdered sugar. Mix until incorporated. Add in spices, and mix until incorporated. Scrape down sides of bowl. Pour in cold heavy cream and vanilla. Whisk on high speed until stiff peaks are achieved and icing holds lines. Add icing to a piping bag with an open star tip. Pipe onto stuffed cupcakes. Garnish each with three toasted mini marshmallows (or one roasted regular marshmallow).

CURE Epilepsy Coconut Caramel
CUPCAKES

> **Whenever I travel to a new city, I try to bake cupcakes for a shelter in that city. In 2019, I was invited to Chicago to share my experience with epilepsy at the Unite to CURE Epilepsy event. While there, I was able to cook with the wonderful folks at Eli's Cheesecake Company, and this was the cupcake I created for that city's donation.**

TIME: 1 HOUR
MAKES: 18 CUPCAKES

CHOCOLATE CUPCAKES
- 2 cups sugar
- 1¾ cups all-purpose flour
- 1 cup unsweetened cocoa powder
- 1½ tsp baking powder
- 1½ tsp baking soda
- 1 tsp salt
- 2 eggs
- 1 cup milk
- ½ cup vegetable oil
- 2 tsp vanilla extract
- 1 cup brewed coffee

CARAMEL
- 2 cups sugar
- ½ cup heavy cream
- 6 tbsp butter
- 1 tsp salt

ICING
- 1 cup heavy cream
- 2 tbsp instant coffee
- 2 cups semisweet chocolate chips

GARNISH
- Toasted coconut flakes (can be bought toasted or toast them yourself)
- Salt

1 Preheat oven to 350°F.

2 For the cupcakes, in a bowl, sift together sugar, flour, cocoa powder, baking powder, baking soda, and salt. Set aside. Whisk together eggs, milk, oil, and vanilla in a separate bowl. Pour wet ingredients in with the dry ingredients. Whisk until completely combined. Add coffee and whisk until completely combined. Line cupcake pans with 18 cupcake liners. Divide batter among liners. Bake for 15 minutes or until a toothpick inserted in the middle comes out clean. Set cupcakes aside to cool.

3 For the caramel, cook sugar in a heavy saucepan over very low heat, stirring frequently, until it melts and turns light brown. Be sure not to burn it, because it browns quickly. Once brown and 340°F to 350°F, remove from heat. Add cream while continuously stirring. Be very careful, it will start to bubble violently. Once it stops bubbling, add butter and salt, stirring until completely combined. Set aside and allow to cool before doing anything with it.

4 For the icing, heat heavy cream and instant coffee in a small heavy saucepan over medium heat until it just starts to lightly simmer. Put chocolate chips into a medium-size metal bowl. Pour hot cream mixture over chocolate chips. Whisk until combined. Pour into a high-sided baking sheet (or sheet cake pan). Put it in the fridge to cool until it has a pudding consistency. Once it is cooled, scrape the chocolate ganache out of the pan and into a stand mixer or use a hand mixer. Using a whisk attachment, whip on medium speed until it is a lighter color and has grown in size.

5 To assemble, use a cupcake corer to core the middle of the cupcake and fill with caramel. Using an ice cream scoop, scoop the whipped icing onto the cupcake. Roll the sides in toasted coconut flakes and drizzle with the caramel, sprinkle with a little salt, and enjoy.

TOASTED COCONUT

You can buy toasted coconut flakes, but you can also toast them yourself. Spread 2 cups coconut flakes in an even layer on a large baking sheet. Bake at 350°F for 8 to 10 minutes, stirring every 2 minutes.

WHAT IS GOLDEN MILK?

Golden milk, also known as turmeric milk, is a bright yellow Indian drink with roots in Ayurveda, one of the world's oldest healing practices. The basic recipe combines animal or plant-based milk with turmeric and other spices, like cinnamon, ginger, and often some kind of sweetener. The recipe you see here was made with these ingredients, as well as black pepper and allspice.

Grandpa Kitchen
GOLDEN MILK CUPCAKES

I was watching YouTube when I came across Grandpa Kitchen, an older gentleman who cooked massive meals for kids in orphanages in India. I was immediately inspired by his actions. He seemed to love the food he made and the kids he helped. I made this cupcake with a homemade golden milk recipe that uses turmeric, pepper, and other spices. Those ingredients might seem unexpected, but trust me, they are delicious together!

TIME: 45 MINUTES
MAKES: 18 CUPCAKES

SPICED CUPCAKES

- 3 cups all-purpose flour
- 1½ tbsp baking powder
- ¾ tsp salt
- 1 tbsp ground turmeric
- ½ tbsp ground cinnamon
- ½ tbsp ground allspice
- ½ tbsp ground ginger
- ½ tbsp ground black pepper
- 1 cup butter, at room temperature
- 2 cups granulated sugar
- 4 eggs
- 1 cup milk
- 1 tsp vanilla

ICING

- 8 ounces cold cream cheese
- 1⅓ cups powdered sugar
- 1 tsp ground turmeric
- ½ tsp ground cinnamon
- ½ tsp ground allspice
- ½ tsp ground ginger
- ½ tsp ground black pepper
- 2 cups cold heavy cream
- 2 tsp vanilla extract

1 Preheat oven to 350°F.

2 For the cupcakes, in a bowl, sift together flour, baking powder, salt, and spices. Set aside. In a stand mixer or using a hand mixer, cream butter until fluffy. Add granulated sugar. Continue to cream for 8 minutes. Add eggs one at a time, making sure they are completely but not overly mixed. Mix in one-third of the flour mixture. Mix the milk and vanilla. Mix in half of the milk mixture (½ cup). Alternate flour mixture and milk, beginning and ending with flour mixture, being careful not to overmix the batter. Line cupcake pans with 18 liners. Divide batter among liners and bake for 15 minutes or until a toothpick inserted in the middle comes out clean. Set cupcakes aside to cool.

3 For the icing, use a whisk attachment on medium speed to whip cream cheese until smooth. Add powdered sugar and spices. Mix. Scrape down the sides of the bowl, pour in cold heavy cream, and whisk on high speed until stiff peaks are achieved and icing holds lines; fold in vanilla. Add icing to a piping bag fitted with a star tip, pipe on the icing, and enjoy!

TURMERIC IS AN INDIAN SPICE THAT COMES FROM A ROOT!

No Kid Hungry
FRENCH TOAST CUPCAKES

TIME: 40 MINUTES
MAKES: 12 CUPCAKES

SPICED FRENCH TOAST CUPCAKES

- ½ cup brown sugar
- 2 tbsp ground cinnamon
- 1¼ cups all-purpose flour
- 1 cup granulated sugar
- ½ cup sour cream
- 4 tbsp butter, melted
- 3 eggs
- 1 tbsp vanilla extract
- 1½ tsp baking powder

MAPLE CREAM CHEESE FROSTING

- 8 ounces cold cream cheese
- 2 tbsp unsalted butter, at room temperature
- ¼ cup cold heavy cream
- 8 ounces frozen whipped topping, thawed
- 1¼ tsp maple extract
- ⅛ tsp salt
- 3 tbsp orange zest

CINNAMON CANDIED BACON

- ¼ cup brown sugar
- ½ tsp ground cinnamon
- 4 slices thick-cut bacon

1 Preheat oven to 350°F.

2 For the cupcakes, mix brown sugar and cinnamon in small bowl. Set aside. Beat remaining ingredients in a large bowl with an electric mixer on low speed just until moistened. Beat on medium speed for 2 minutes.

3 Line a cupcake pan with 12 liners. Spoon half of the batter evenly into muffin cups. Sprinkle 2 tsp of brown sugar–cinnamon mixture over batter in each cup. Spoon remaining batter evenly over top.

4 Bake for 15 to 17 minutes or until a toothpick inserted into the center of a cupcake comes out with moist crumbs. Cool in pan for 5 minutes. Remove from pan. Cool completely on a wire rack.

5 For the frosting, beat cream cheese and butter in a large bowl until smooth. Add heavy cream. Beat until light and fluffy. Stir in whipped topping, maple extract, and salt. Beat until stiff peaks form. Pipe or spread frosting onto cooled cupcakes. Sprinkle cupcakes with orange zest and candied bacon (see box, facing page).

No Kid Hungry is an initiative that helps provide support for children and families who are experiencing food insecurity. One program that they support is called Breakfast in the Classroom. This important program provides schools with grants to make sure every kid gets breakfast. My cupcake recipe was created in collaboration with the chefs at McCormick & Company, and is an ode to that initiative. It's a French toast cupcake with maple icing, candied bacon, and orange zest. Breakfast for dessert!

CINNAMON CANDIED BACON

Preheat oven to 375°F. Mix brown sugar and cinnamon in small bowl. Coat bacon with cinnamon-sugar mixture. Arrange bacon slices in single layer on foil-lined 15" x 10" x 1" baking pan. Bake for 10 to 15 minutes or until brown and crisp. Cool before crumbling.

Chef José Andrés started World Central Kitchen to help provide meals to areas that are experiencing crisis. That crisis may be a weather event like a hurricane or some other event that creates displaced people who need meals. WCK is important to me because it helps people when they need it most.

ARROZ CON LECHE

José Andrés is not only a chef and humanitarian, but he's also a native of Spain. Arroz con leche (rice pudding) is a popular Spanish dish he has featured in cookbooks and at restaurants.

José Andrés
ARROZ CON LECHE CUPCAKES

TIME: 45 MINUTES
MAKES: 24 CUPCAKES

CUPCAKES

- 3 cups all-purpose flour
- 1½ tbsp baking powder
- ¾ tsp salt
- 1 cup butter, at room temperature
- 2 cups granulated sugar
- 4 eggs
- 1 cup milk
- 1 tsp vanilla extract

RICE PUDDING FILLING

- ½ cup medium-grain white rice
- 1 cup water
- 2 cinnamon sticks
- 3 cups milk
- 1 egg yolk
- 3 tbsp butter
- 2 tsp vanilla extract
- ½ cup granulated sugar
- Pinch of salt

GARNISH

- 1 cup brown sugar

1 Preheat oven to 350°F.

2 For the cupcakes, in a bowl, sift together flour, baking powder, and salt. Set aside. In a stand mixer or with a hand mixer, cream butter until fluffy. Add granulated sugar and continue to cream for 8 minutes. Add eggs one at a time, making sure they are completely but not overly mixed. Add one-third of the flour mixture and mix. Combine the milk and vanilla. Mix in half the milk mixture (½ cup) with the batter. Alternate flour mixture and milk, beginning and ending with flour, being careful not to overmix the batter. Line cupcake pans with 24 paper liners. Divide batter among liners. Bake for 15 minutes or until a toothpick inserted into the middle of a cupcake comes out clean. Let the cupcakes cool.

3 For the rice pudding filling, place rice, water, and cinnamon sticks in a medium pot over medium heat. Cook according to rice package directions until the rice is soft and paste-like (about 15 to 30 minutes depending on your rice). Drain water and remove cinnamon sticks. Set aside the cooked rice. In a separate pot, bring milk to a boil over high heat, being careful not to let it scorch. Add cooked rice, lower to medium heat, and use a wooden spoon to stir continually. Be sure not to let the rice burn. When the consistency of the rice coats the back of a wooden spoon, remove the pot from the heat. In a small bowl, beat the egg yolk and stir in a spoonful of the rice mixture. Mix one more spoonful of the rice mixture into the egg yolk and add the mixture back into the rice, stirring continuously. Add butter a bit at a time. Stir in completely. The mixture should be creamy and thick enough to coat the back of a wooden spoon. Stir in the vanilla and granulated sugar. Taste and adjust with a pinch of salt, if needed.

4 When the cupcakes are cool, core out the center of each cupcake and fill to the top with rice pudding. Top each with a generous portion of brown sugar. Place under a broiler for a few minutes to brown, but be sure to watch carefully so the tops don't burn.

Harriet Tubman
MINT CHOCOLATE CUPCAKES

TIME: 45 MINUTES
MAKES: 18 CUPCAKES

CUPCAKES

- 2 cups granulated sugar
- 1¾ cups all-purpose flour
- 1 cup unsweetened cocoa powder
- 1½ tsp baking powder
- 1½ tsp baking soda
- 1 tsp salt
- 2 eggs
- 1 cup milk
- ½ cup vegetable oil
- 2 tsp vanilla extract
- 1 cup boiling water

ICING

- 8 ounces cold cream cheese
- 1⅓ cups powdered sugar
- 2 cups cold heavy cream
- 1 tsp mint extract
- ¼ cup unsweetened cocoa powder

GARNISH (OPTIONAL)
Small mint leaves

1 Preheat oven to 350°F.

2 For the cupcakes, in a bowl, sift together granulated sugar, flour, cocoa powder, baking powder, baking soda, and salt. Set aside. In a separate bowl, whisk together eggs, milk, oil, and vanilla. Pour the wet ingredients in with the dry ingredients. Whisk until completely combined. Add boiling water. Whisk until completely combined. Line cupcake pans with 18 liners. Divide batter among liners. Bake for 15 minutes or until a toothpick inserted in the middle of a cupcake comes out clean. Set cupcakes aside to cool.

3 For the icing, using the whisk attachment with a stand mixer or hand mixer, whisk cream cheese on medium speed until smooth. Add powdered sugar. Mix. Scrape down the sides of the bowl. Pour in cold heavy cream. Whisk on high speed until stiff peaks are achieved. Transfer half the icing to a separate bowl. Add mint extract. Fold until completely combined. To the remaining icing in the stand mixer bowl, add cocoa powder and whip on medium speed until it is completely combined. Place a layer of plastic wrap on a flat surface. Scoop one line of each icing (mint and chocolate) onto the plastic wrap, then roll the plastic wrap up into a log. Put the icing log into a piping bag with an open star tip and pipe onto cupcakes. Garnish with a small mint leaf, if desired.

Leah Chase
BUTTER CAKE CUPCAKES

Leah Chase was an amazing chef and civil rights activist based in New Orleans who offered her upscale restaurant space as a gathering place for other civil rights activists in the mid-twentieth century and played her part in sustaining the movement! This is a cupcake based on one of her recipes, Butter Cake.

TIME: 45 MINUTES
MAKES: 18 CUPCAKES

- 1 pound salted butter, at room temperature
- 2 cups granulated sugar
- 6 eggs
- 2 tsp vanilla extract
- 6 tbsp milk
- 2 cups all-purpose flour
- ½ cup powdered sugar
  Melted butter and flour for greasing cupcake pan
  Brown sugar for topping

1 Preheat oven to 350°F.

2 In the bowl of a stand mixer with a whisk attachment or with a hand mixer, whisk the softened butter until smooth. Add granulated sugar and whip until smooth, then add one egg at a time while whipping. Add vanilla and milk. Whip until smooth. Add flour and powdered sugar. Using a paddle attachment on low speed, whip until completely combined. Be careful not to overmix. Brush melted butter into 18 cupcake pan cups, then coat with flour. Divide batter among liners, and bake on the middle rack of the oven for 20 minutes or until a toothpick inserted in the middle of a cupcake comes out clean.

3 Take the cupcakes out of the oven, and set the oven to broil. Sprinkle with a generous amount of brown sugar and put back in the oven about 4" from the heat for 2 minutes, or until the brown sugar is melted. Set cupcakes aside to cool.

Malala Yousafzai
CARROT HALWA CUPCAKES

TIME: 45 MINUTES
MAKES: 18 CUPCAKES

CARROT HALWA FILLING

- 1 tsp cardamom
- 1 tbsp salted butter
- 1½ cups grated carrots
- ½ cup milk
- ¼ cup condensed milk

SPICED CUPCAKES

- 3¼ cups all-purpose flour, divided
- 1½ tbsp baking powder
- ¾ tsp salt
- 1 tsp ground cardamom
- 1 cup butter, at room temperature
- 2 cups granulated sugar
- 4 eggs
- 1 cup milk
- 1 tsp vanilla extract
- ¾ cup raisins

ICING AND GARNISH

- 8 ounces cold cream cheese
- 1⅓ cups powdered sugar
- 2 cups cold heavy cream
- 1 tsp vanilla extract
- ½ cup pistachios

1 Preheat oven to 350°F.

2 For the cupcake filling, in a dry pan over medium-high heat, toast cardamom until fragrant, being sure not to burn it. Add butter and melt completely. Add carrots and cook until they just start to brown a little bit. Add milk and cook until most of it has evaporated. Add condensed milk. Cook until mostly evaporated. Remove from the heat and set aside.

3 For the cupcakes, in a bowl, sift together 3 cups of the flour, baking powder, salt, and ground cardamom. Set aside. In a stand mixer or with a hand mixer, cream butter until fluffy. Add granulated sugar. Continue to cream for 8 minutes. Add eggs one at a time, making sure they're completely but not overly mixed. Mix in one-third of the flour mix. Combine milk and vanilla. Add half the milk mixture (½ cup) to the batter. Mix. Alternate flour mixture and milk, beginning and ending with flour. Be careful not to overmix the batter.

4 In a small bowl, mix raisins and remaining ¼ cup flour until the raisins are coated. Set aside. Line cupcake pans with 18 paper liners. Put about 1 tbsp raisins into each empty cupcake liner. Divide batter among liners (half to two-thirds full). Bake for 15 minutes or until a toothpick inserted into the middle of a cupcake comes out clean. Let cool.

5 For the icing, using the whisk attachment of a stand mixer or a handmixer, whip cream cheese on medium speed until smooth. Add powdered sugar and mix. Scrape down the sides of the bowl, pour in cold heavy cream, and whisk on high speed until stiff peaks are achieved and icing holds lines. Fold in vanilla. Core out the middle of each cupcake with a cupcake corer and stuff with some of the carrot halwa. Pipe on some icing, top with whole or crushed pistachios, and enjoy!

This cupcake is dedicated to a really inspiring woman, Malala Yousafzai, a Pakistani education advocate who promotes equality for girls and access to education worldwide. Carrot halwa is a very popular dessert in Pakistan and it makes me think of carrot cake . . . but better! I decided it would be a great idea to stuff a cupcake with carrot halwa, then top it with sweet cream cheese frosting and pistachios. I also happen to know that, like me, Malala loves sweets!

Booker T. Washington was an American educator, author, speaker, and adviser to many presidents. He was born into slavery and emancipated in 1865 when the Civil War ended. He put himself through school and started the Tuskegee Institute in 1881, which focused on training newly emancipated Black people to be teachers, farmers, and entrepreneurs so that they could provide for themselves. He felt this was the best way for Black people to reclaim the mostly rural communities of the South. This plant-based cupcake is in honor of the skills Booker T. Washington used to empower his community.

Booker T. Washington
VEGAN CHOCOLATE CUPCAKES

TIME: 1 HOUR 30 MINUTES
MAKES: 18 CUPCAKES

CHOCOLATE CUPCAKES

- 1 tbsp milled fllax
- 3 tbsp water
- 2 cups granulated sugar
- 1¾ cups all-purpose flour
- 1 cup unsweetened cocoa powder
- 1½ tsp baking powder
- 1½ tsp baking soda
- 1 tsp salt
- 1 cup almond milk
- ½ cup vegetable oil
- 2 tsp vanilla extract
- ¼ cup applesauce
- 1 cup boiling water

CHOCOLATE-COFFEE ICING

- ½ tsp instant coffee
- ⅓ cup almond milk
- 1½ tsp vanilla extract
- ½ cup vegan butter, at room temperature
- 1 cup unsweetened cocoa powder
- 2½ cups powdered sugar

1 Preheat oven to 350°F.

2 For the cupcakes, in a small bowl, combine flax and water, stir, and set aside. In a large bowl, sift together granulated sugar, flour, cocoa powder, baking powder, baking soda, and salt. Set aside. In a separate bowl, whisk together flax mixture, almond milk, oil, vanilla, and applesauce. Pour the wet ingredients in with the dry ingredients and whisk until completely combined. Add the water and whisk until completely combined.

3 Line a cupcake pan with cupcake liners. Divide the batter among the liners and bake for 15 minutes or until a toothpick inserted in the middle of a cupcake comes out clean. Set aside to cool.

4 For the icing, in a cup, dissolve instant coffee in almond milk. Add vanilla and set aside. Add butter, cocoa powder, and powdered sugar to a stand mixer or use a hand mixer and begin to mix. Add almond milk mixture and continue to whip until it reaches the desired consistency. Add more almond milk if the icing is too thick. Add more powdered sugar if it's too thin.

5 Fill a piping bag fitted with a star tip and pipe on the icing. Enjoy!

Nelson Mandela
MALVA PUDDING CUPCAKES

TIME: 45 MINUTES
MAKES: 18 CUPCAKES

MALVA CREAM SAUCE

½ cup milk
½ cup heavy cream
¼ cup unsweetened cocoa powder
¼ cup granulated sugar
1 tsp ground cinnamon

CUPCAKES

3 cups all-purpose flour
1½ tbsp baking powder
¾ tsp salt
1 cup butter, at room temperature
2 cups granulated sugar
4 eggs
1 cup milk

ICING

8 ounces cold cream cheese
1⅓ cups powdered sugar
2 cups cold heavy cream
1 tsp vanilla extract
¼ cup unsweetened cocoa powder

Nelson Mandela was a South African anti-apartheid freedom fighter and the first democratically elected president of South Africa. He did a lot of work around civil rights and anti-colonialism in his country. He went to prison for twenty-seven years for opposing the country's segregation laws before he was freed and became president. He's inspiring to me because he worked passionately around one issue until it was solved, even when there were so many things in his way and people trying to stop him.

1 Preheat oven to 350°F.

2 For the cream sauce, continually whisk together all of the ingredients in a pot over medium heat until it becomes steamy but not boiling, and sugar is dissolved. Set aside but keep warm.

3 For the cupcakes, in a bowl, sift together flour, baking powder, and salt. Set aside. In a stand mixer or with a hand mixer, cream butter until fluffy. Add granulated sugar. Continue to cream for 8 minutes. Add eggs one at a time, making sure they're completely but not overly mixed. Mix in one-third of the flour mixture. Add half the milk (½ cup) to the batter and mix. Alternate flour mixture and milk, beginning and ending with flour, being careful not to overmix the batter. Line cupcake pans with 18 paper cupcake liners. Divide batter among liners (half to two-thirds full). Bake for 15 minutes or until a toothpick inserted into the middle of a cupcake comes out clean. Set cupcakes aside to cool. Poke a few holes in them with a fork or chopstick and pour 2 tbsp of the cream sauce over each cupcake.

4 For the icing, using a stand mixer fitted a whisk attachment or a hand mixer, whip the cream cheese on medium speed until smooth. Add powdered sugar and mix until incorporated. Scrape down the sides of the bowl, pour in cold heavy cream, and whisk on high speed until stiff peaks are achieved and icing holds lines. Fold in vanilla. Pipe on some icing, sprinkle on unsweetened cocoa powder to garnish, and enjoy!

WHAT IS MALVA PUDDING?

Malva pudding is a South African baked dessert that traditionally contains apricot jam, but chocolate versions are also popular! The warm cream sauce is poured over the cake immediately after it comes hot out of the oven.

LEMON MERINGUE PIE

2

Pies & Tarts

Pies are a great way to use in-season fruits and play with new flavors. They're very versatile! You can make fruit pies, custard pies, hand pies, hot, cold, baked, fried, etc. All are delicious, and if you know how to make some pies, you should have no trouble making all of them. Pies are a big part of my baking arsenal and experience, especially sweet potato pie.

SWEET POTATO PIE

TIME: 1 HOUR 30 MINUTES
MAKES: ONE 9" PIE*

FILLING

- 1 pound sweet potatoes
- ½ cup butter, melted
- ½ cup granulated sugar
- ½ cup brown sugar
- ½ cup heavy cream
- 1 egg
- 1 tsp ground cinnamon
- ½ tsp ground nutmeg
- ¼ tsp ground cloves
- 1 tsp vanilla extract

CRUST

- 1⅓ cups all-purpose flour
- 1 tbsp powdered sugar
- ¼ tsp salt
- 7 tbsp cold unsalted butter
- 1 egg yolk
- 2 to 3 tbsp ice cold water

Sweet potato pie is one of the most important desserts I can think of. Sweet potatoes were introduced to the United States by way of the Caribbean and recognized by enslaved Africans as akin to their West African yams. Sweet potato pie is one of the first desserts that I can ever remember. The recipe has been passed down for generations, and through experience has been slightly tweaked over the decades. Here is my version.

1 Preheat oven to 350°F.

2 To start the filling, poke the sweet potatoes a few times each with a fork, and roast on a foil-lined baking sheet until they're soft and oozing sap (about an hour). Let cool.

3 Make the crust while the sweet potatoes are roasting. In a bowl, sift together flour, powdered sugar, and salt. Cube cold butter. Press it into flour mixture using your fingertips until the consistency of sand is created. Beat egg yolk and water together in a small bowl. Add it to the flour mix. Combine until a dough is formed. Knead the dough until it just comes together. Wrap the dough in plastic wrap and let it rest for 30 minutes in the refrigerator. Once rested, roll out the dough to a ¼" thick round big enough to have excess when placed in your 9" pie pan. Place the crust in your pie pan, trim and crimp the edges, and set aside.

4 Continue the filling. Once the sweet potatoes are cool enough to handle, peel their skins off (they should slide right off). Place in a large bowl. Add butter, sugars, cream, egg, cinnamon, nutmeg, cloves, and vanilla. Mix with a whisk or hand mixer until smooth. Pour the filling into your pie shell. Bake for 50 to 60 minutes.

*Mini pies (as seen on the left) are a fun way to switch up how pies are served. Remember to keep an eye on them though, because they will cook a little bit faster.

BROWN SUGAR PIE

TIME: 1 HOUR, 30 MINUTES
MAKES: TWO 9" PIES

CLASSIC CRUST (YIELDS 2 CRUSTS)

- 2⅔ cups all-purpose flour
- 2 tbsp powdered sugar
- ½ tsp salt
- 1 cup cold, unsalted butter, cubed
- 2 egg yolks
- 4 to 6 tbsp ice cold water

FILLING

- 3 eggs
- 2 cups light brown sugar
- ½ cup unsalted butter, melted
- 1 tbsp vanilla extract

While it originally appears to be European in origin, brown sugar pie is popular throughout the United States, including the South. It may not be the most commonly known dessert, but it's an old-fashioned favorite that is so good! Serve it with ice cream or whipped cream on top for a delicious treat anytime. You could even eat it for breakfast!

1. Preheat oven to 350°F.

2. For the crust, in a stand mixer with the paddle attachment or with a hand mixer, combine flour, powdered sugar, salt, and butter until there are only small clumps of butter. In a separate bowl, combine egg yolks and water. Pour egg mix into flour mix, and mix on medium speed until a dough forms. Divide dough in half. Wrap in plastic wrap and put in fridge for 30 minutes. Remove from fridge. Roll out into a rough circle on a floured surface, about ¼" thick and big enough to have excess when placed in a 9" pie pan. Lay dough into pans. Cut off excess and crimp edges. Set both crusts aside.

3. For the filling, in a bowl, whisk eggs. Add brown sugar, melted butter, and vanilla. Whisk until just combined. Be careful not to overmix.

4. To assemble, pour the filling evenly into the two pans and bake for 45 to 50 minutes or until set up. Allow to cool completely before cutting.

CHOCOLATE PIE

TIME: 1 HOUR 30 MINUTES
(PLUS TIME FOR CHILLING)
MAKES: ONE 9" PIE

CRUST
- 1⅓ cups all-purpose flour
- 2 tbsp powdered sugar
- ¼ tsp salt
- 1 egg yolk
- ½ cup cold unsalted butter
- 3 to 4tbsp ice water

FILLING
- 3 tbsp cornstarch
- ¾ cup granulated sugar
- ⅛ tsp salt
- 1½ cups milk
- 3 egg yolks
- 1 tsp instant coffee
- 1 cup semisweet chocolate chips
- 1 tsp vanilla extract
- 2 tbsp butter

WHIPPED CREAM
- 1 cup heavy cream
- ½ cup powdered sugar
- 1 tsp vanilla extract

GARNISH (OPTIONAL)
Grated chocolate

1 For the crust, combine flour, powdered sugar, and salt in a bowl. Cut in butter until a sandy mixture is achieved. Mix egg yolk and water in a small bowl. Sprinkle over flour mixture and knead until dough comes together, sprinkling on more water if dough is still too dry. Wrap in plastic wrap and put in the fridge for 2 hours up to overnight.

2 Preheat oven to 350°F.

3 After the dough is chilled, roll it out on a floured work surface into a ¼" thick round big enough to have excess when placed in a 9" pie pan. Place the crust in the pie pan and trim and crimp the edges. Prick crust with a fork and bake for 12 minutes. Set aside to cool.

4 For the filling, in a medium pot, whisk together cornstarch, granulated sugar, and salt. Add milk, egg yolks, and instant coffee and place over medium heat. Whisk until it starts to thicken. Once it thickens to a pudding consistency and starts slightly bubbling, remove from heat. Whisk in chocolate chips, vanilla, and butter. Pour into the pie crust and put in the fridge for 4 hours.

5 For the whipped cream, put the bowl of a stand mixer and the whisk attachment into the freezer for about 10 minutes. Remove from the freezer, and pour the heavy cream into the bowl. Whip on medium speed. Slowly add powdered sugar. Once all is added turn the speed up to high and whip until you have stiff peaks.

6 Remove pie from the fridge, top with the whipped cream, and sprinkle with grated chocolate.

Coffee Chocolate
MOUSSE PIE

TIME: 1 HOUR 30 MINUTES
(PLUS TIME FOR CHILLING)
MAKES: ONE 9" PIE*

GRAHAM CRACKER CRUST
- 2 cups graham cracker crumbs
- ½ cup salted butter, melted
- ½ cup granulated sugar

COFFEE CHOCOLATE MOUSSE
- 1 cup semisweet chocolate chips
- ½ cup salted butter
- 2 tbsp instant coffee
- 8 eggs, separated
- ½ cup granulated sugar
- 1 cup heavy cream

WHIPPED CREAM TOPPING
- 1 cup heavy cream
- ½ cup powdered sugar
- 1 tsp vanilla extract

> **Chocolate mousse is one of the first things that I ever learned how to make! I have developed the recipe over the years, adding coffee, changing the consistency, and experimenting with toppings. This is absolutely one of my favorite desserts and is pretty easy if you are willing to wait for it to set up.**

1 Preheat oven to 350°F.

2 For the crust, pour all ingredients into a bowl. Stir until it forms a wet sand-like texture, making sure there are no dry patches or wet, soggy patches. Pour and press into a 9" pie pan, making sure it's even all the way around. Bake for 10 minutes or until it has slightly browned. Set aside to cool until you're ready to use it.

3 For the mousse, in the top of a double boiler, melt chocolate chips, butter, and instant coffee. Once melted and combined, add egg yolks. Whisk until smooth, being sure not to cook the eggs. Set aside to cool. Pour egg whites into the bowl of a stand mixer or use a hand mixer. Using a whisk attachment, whip egg whites on low speed for 2 minutes. Add granulated sugar, turn the speed up to medium, and whip for another 2 minutes. Turn the speed up to high, and whip for another 2 minutes until stiff peaks form. In a separate bowl, whip heavy cream until you have stiff peaks. In a big bowl, combine the chocolate mixture and half the whipped cream. Mix until combined. Add the rest of the whipped cream and all the whipped egg whites. Fold together until combined, being sure not to deflate the mixture. Pour it into the prepared pie crust. Put into the fridge for about 2 hours or until set up.

4 For the whipped cream topping, put the bowl of a stand mixer and whisk attachment into the freezer for about 10 minutes. Remove from the freezer and pour the heavy cream into the bowl. Whip on medium speed. Slowly add powdered sugar. Once all the powdered sugar is added turn the speed up to high and whip until you have stiff peaks.

5 To assemble, remove the mousse pie from the fridge, top with the whipped cream, and enjoy.

*Mini pies (as seen on the right) are a fun way to switch up how pies are served. Remember to keep an eye on them though, because they will cook a little bit faster.

KEY LIME PIE

TIME: 1 HOUR 30 MINUTES
(PLUS TIME FOR COOLING)
MAKES: ONE 9" PIE

GRAHAM CRACKER CRUST
1½ cups graham cracker crumbs
5 tbsp butter, melted
¼ cup granulated sugar

KEY LIME PIE FILLING
3 egg yolks
1 tbsp lime zest
1¾ cups sweetened condensed milk
⅔ cup Key lime juice

WHIPPED CREAM
1 cup heavy cream
½ cup powdered sugar

1 Preheat oven to 350°F.

2 For the crust, pour all of the ingredients into a bowl and stir until it forms a wet sand-like texture, making sure there are no dry patches or wet and soggy patches. Pour and press into a 9" pie pan, making sure it's even all the way around. Bake for 10 minutes or until it has slightly browned. Set aside to cool but leave the oven on.

3 For the filling, in a stand mixer with a whisk attachment or with a hand mixer, whisk
egg yolks and lime zest until lighter in color and slightly airy. Add condensed milk and lime juice. Whisk until combined. Cover with plastic wrap and let it rest for 30 minutes. Pour the filling into the pie crust and bake for about 20 minutes or until set up but still jiggly. Remove from oven and let cool at room temperature for 20 minutes, then place in the fridge for 4 hours.

4 For the whipped cream, put the bowl of a stand mixer and the whisk attachment into the freezer for about 10 minutes. Remove from the freezer and pour the heavy cream into the bowl and whip on medium speed. Slowly add the powdered sugar. Once all is added turn the speed up to high and whip until you have stiff peaks.

5 Remove the pie from the fridge, top with whipped cream, and sprinkle with lime zest.

BOTTLED KEY LIME JUICE OR FRESH?

Bottled key lime juice is milder and less acidic than fresh lime juice and it's available at most groceries and online. However, if you can use fresh lime juice, give it a try for its brighter, more intense flavor!

LEMON MERINGUE TART

TIME: 1 HOUR 30 MINUTES
MAKES: ONE 9" PIE*

CRUST

1⅓ cups all-purpose flour
1 tbsp powdered sugar
⅛ tsp salt
½ cup cold unsalted butter, cubed
1 egg yolk
2 to 3 tbsp water

LEMON CURD FILLING

¾ cup lemon juice
2 tbsp lemon zest
¾ cup granulated sugar
3 egg yolks
½ cup unsalted butter
2 tbsp cornstarch

MERINGUE

3 egg whites, at room temperature
¾ cup granulated sugar
⅛ tsp cream of tartar

1 Preheat oven to 350°F.

2 For the crust, in a stand mixer using the paddle attachment or with a hand mixer, combine flour, powdered sugar, salt, and butter until there are only small clumps of butter. In a separate bowl, combine egg yolk and 2 tbsp water. Pour egg mix into flour mixture, and mix on medium speed until a dough forms. Add another 1 tbsp of water if dough seems dry. Wrap in plastic wrap, and put in the fridge for 30 minutes. Remove from fridge. On a floured surface, roll into a rough circle big enough to fit into your tart pan. Put into your pan. Dock (poke holes) in the bottom of the pie pan with a fork and bake for 10 minutes or until golden brown. Remove from the oven and let cool. Turn the oven up to 400°F.

3 For the filling, in a pot, combine lemon juice, zest, granulated sugar, egg yolks, butter, and cornstarch. Place over medium heat and whisk until the butter melts. Once melted, turn up heat to medium-high and whisk continuously until it thickens. Once thickened, pour into a bowl and cover with plastic wrap or a butter wrapper. Be sure it touches the surface of the curd so a film won't develop. Store in the fridge until you're ready to use it.

4 For the meringue, pour the egg whites into the bowl of a stand mixer or use a hand mixer. Using the whisk attachment, whip on low speed for 2 minutes. Add the granulated sugar and cream of tartar. Turn the speed to medium and whip for another 2 minutes. Turn the speed up to high and whip until you have stiff peaks.

5 Pour the lemon curd filling into the crust. Spread it out evenly with a spoon or rubber spatula. Scoop or pipe the meringue on top. Turn on the broiler and broil long enough to brown the meringue. This won't take long at all, so watch it and don't walk away! Slice and enjoy!

*This recipe yields one 9" pie or four 4" mini pies (like the mini pie shown at right). Mini pies bake a little faster, so keep an eye on them.

PEACH COBBLER TART

TIME: 1 HOUR 30 MINUTES
(PLUS TIME TO CHILL THE DOUGH)
MAKES: ONE 9" PIE*

CLASSIC CRUST

- ½ cup cold unsalted butter, cubed
- 1 tbsp powdered sugar
- ½ tsp salt
- 1 egg yolk
- 1⅓ cups all-purpose flour2 to 3 tbsp water

FILLING

- 8 peaches, peeled, pitted, and sliced
- 4 tbsp butter, melted
- 2 tsp cornstarch
- ½ cup brown sugar
- ¼ cup granulated sugar
- 1 tsp ground cinnamon
- ½ tsp ground nutmeg
- ½ tsp ground allspice

1 For the crust, in a stand mixer with a paddle attachment or with a hand mixer, combine butter, sugar, and salt. Mix on medium speed until combined. Add egg yolk. Mix. Add flour and water. Mix until you have a dough. Wrap in plastic wrap and put in the fridge for 2 hours or overnight. Roll out your dough (leaving some for a lattice on top), line your tart pan with it, and dock (poke holes) in the bottom with a fork.

2 Preheat oven to 350°F. Bake for 10 minutes. Once done, set on a cooling rack to cool.

3 For the filling, in a bowl, mix together the peaches, butter, cornstarch, brown sugar, granulated sugar, cinnamon, nutmeg, and allspice.

4 Fill your tart shell with the peach mixture. Place a lattice on top and bake until golden brown, about 35 minutes. Remove from the oven and let cool. Cut and enjoy.

*Mini pies (as seen on the left) are a fun way to switch up how pies are served. Remember to keep an eye on them though, because they will cook a little bit faster.

> My great-grandparents had their own farm, garden, and hogs. Every year, once peaches came into season, they would lend their rooster to neighbors in turn for a few bushels of peaches from their orchards. Every year, my great-grandma Sarah E. would make buttery peach cobbler and preserve the rest by canning them to enjoy after the season.

FRESH PEACHES

In the United States, summer's the time when peaches are in season, so this is a recipe you might want to try in July or August, when they're at their best from your local farmers' market or grocery store.

Chess pie is from the South, and the origin of its name is uncertain. One story is that a cook on a plantation made it, and when asked what she'd made, she answered, "Just pie," which in a Southern accent could have been misheard as "chess pie."

CHESS PIE

TIME: 1 HOUR 30 MINUTES
MAKES: ONE 9" PIE

CLASSIC CRUST

- 1⅓ cups all-purpose flour
- 1 tbsp powdered sugar
- ½ tsp salt
- 7 tbsp cold unsalted butter, cubed
- 1 egg yolk
- 2 tbsp water

FILLING

- ½ cup butter
- 2 cups granulated sugar
- 2 tsp vanilla extract
- 4 eggs
- 1 tbsp cornmeal
- ¼ cup evaporated milk
- 1 tbsp apple cider vinegar

GARNISH

Powdered sugar, for dusting

1 Preheat the oven to 425°F.

2 For the crust, in a stand mixer with a paddle attachment or with a hand mixer, combine flour, powdered sugar, salt, and butter until there are only small clumps of butter. In a separate bowl, combine egg yolk and water. Pour the egg mixture into the flour mixture and mix on medium speed until a dough forms. Wrap in plastic wrap and put in the fridge for 30 minutes. Remove from the fridge and roll out into a rough circle, big enough for your pan, on a floured surface. Put into a pie pan and set aside.

3 For the filling, in a large bowl, mix butter, granulated sugar, and vanilla until combined. Add eggs and whisk until combined. Stir in cornmeal, milk, and vinegar until smooth. Pour into the prepared crust.

4 Bake at 425°F for 10 minutes, then lower to 300°F and bake for 40 minutes. Cover with foil if it starts to get too brown. Turn off oven and let cool in oven. Remove once completely cooled. Dust with powdered sugar.

ABOUT CORNMEAL

Cornmeal is a very important ingredient in both African and Indigenous culinary traditions. Cornmeal is what gives chess pie it's delicious flavor and texture.

COCONUT CREAM PIE

TIME: 1 HOUR 30 MINUTES
MAKES: ONE 9" PIE*

GARNISH
- ⅓ cup flaked coconut

GRAHAM CRACKER CRUST
- 2 cups graham cracker crumbs
- ½ cup butter, melted
- ½ cup granulated sugar

FILLING
- 1 13.5-ounce can coconut cream, refrigerated
- 3 egg yolks
- ¾ cup granulated sugar
- ¼ cup cornstarch
- ¼ tsp salt
- 2 cups half-and-half
- ⅔ cup flaked coconut
- 1 tsp vanilla extract

WHIPPED CREAM
- 1 cup heavy whipping cream, refrigerated
- ½ cup powdered sugar
- 1 tsp vanilla extract

1 Preheat oven to 350°F.

2 For the garnish, toast ⅓ cup coconut flakes in a small pan over medium heat. Be sure to keep the flakes moving and watch them carefully to avoid burning. Stop toasting when the coconut is golden brown. Set aside to cool.

3 For the crust, pour all ingredients into a bowl. Stir until it forms a wet sand-like texture, making sure there are no dry patches or wet, soggy patches. Pour and press into a 9" pie pan, making sure it's even all the way around. Bake for 10 minutes or until it has slightly browned. Set aside to cool until you're ready to use it.

4 For the filling, skim the coconut cream from the top of the can (being careful to leave the remaining water in the can). Place in a medium saucepan. Whisk in egg yolks, granulated sugar, cornstarch, and salt. Whisk in the half-and-half. Cook over medium heat, whisking continuously, until the curd thickens. Remove from heat. Add raw coconut flakes and vanilla. Pour the curd into the prepared pie shell and set aside.

5 To make the whipped cream, first make sure the cream is very cold. If you can chill your mixing bowl and whisk attachment, that will also help your cream whip up. Place all ingredients into the bowl of a stand mixer or use a hand mixer and mix on medium-high speed until stiff peaks form.

6 Top the pie with the whipped cream, then toasted flaked coconut.

*Mini pies (as seen on the right) are a fun way to switch up how pies are served. Remember to keep an eye on them though, because they will cook a little bit faster.

ABOUT COCONUT

Coconut is used for both the filling and the garnish in this recipe. Not only has coconut been an ingredient in tasty desserts like this one for many years, but it's also packed with nutrients, so it's good for you!

Mixed
BERRY PIE

TIME: 1 HOUR 30 MINUTES
(PLUS TIME FOR THE PIE TO COOL)
MAKES: ONE 9" PIE

CLASSIC CRUST
(YIELDS 2 CRUSTS)

2⅔ cups all-purpose flour
 2 tbsp powdered sugar
 ½ tsp salt
 1 cup cold unsalted butter, cubed
 2 egg yolks
 4 to 6 tbsp water
 1 egg, beaten, for brushing dough
   Cane sugar or sanding sugar, for sprinkling (optional)

FILLING

 1 cup fresh or frozen strawberries, cut in half
 2 cups fresh or frozen raspberries
 2 cups fresh or frozen blueberries
 ¾ cup granulated sugar
 ¼ cup cornstarch
 1 tsp ground cinnamon
   Zest of ½ lemon

1 For the crust, in a stand mixer with a paddle attachment or with a hand mixer, combine flour, powdered sugar, salt, and butter until there are only small clumps of butter. Change paddle attachment to a dough hook. In a separate bowl, combine egg yolk and water. Pour the egg mixture into the flour mixture and mix on medium speed until a dough forms. Split the dough into two balls. Wrap in plastic wrap. Put in the fridge for 1 hour. Remove from the fridge. Roll one ball out into a rough circle, big enough to fit your pie pan, on a floured surface. Put into a pie pan and set aside. Roll the other dough out to use for the top crust of the pie.

2 Preheat oven to 350°F.

3 For the filling, place fruit, granulated sugar, cornstarch, cinnamon, and lemon zest in a large bowl. Toss to thoroughly coat.

4 Pour the fruit mixture into the prepared pie pan. Top with the second pie dough and crimp the edges together. Brush the top of the pie with beaten egg. Cut four or five 2" slits in the top of the pie crust. Cover with foil. Bake for 30 minutes. Remove the foil and bake for an additional 30 minutes. Allow to cool overnight so the pie can set up. Enjoy!

Optional: After brushing on the egg wash you can dust the top with whole cane sugar or sanding sugar.

ZESTING TOOL

ZESTING CITRUS FRUITS

Zest is the outermost portion of a citrus fruit's peel. It's often used to add tangy flavor to recipes such as pies. There are special tools for zesting citrus fruit, but if you have a good vegetable peeler or paring knife, it can do a great job of removing the zest. Just remove the zest in large strips from the fruit, then finely mince if needed. Just make sure you only get the zest, not any of the pith (the white part underneath the zest), which is bitter.

PECAN PIE

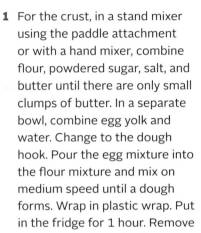

TIME: 1 HOUR 30 MINUTES
MAKES: ONE 9" PIE*

CRUST
- 1⅓ cups all-purpose flour
- 1 tbsp powdered sugar
- ¼ tsp salt
- 1 cup cold unsalted butter, cubed
- 1 egg yolk
- 2 to 3 tbsp cold water

FILLING
- 3 eggs
- 1 egg yolk
- ¼ cup maple syrup
- 1 cup corn syrup
- ¾ tsp salt
- ¾ cup brown sugar
- 1 tbsp vanilla extract
- 4 tbsp butter, melted
- 1 tsp ground cinnamon
- 3 cups chopped pecans

GARNISH
- 1 to 2 cups whole pecans

1 For the crust, in a stand mixer using the paddle attachment or with a hand mixer, combine flour, powdered sugar, salt, and butter until there are only small clumps of butter. In a separate bowl, combine egg yolk and water. Change to the dough hook. Pour the egg mixture into the flour mixture and mix on medium speed until a dough forms. Wrap in plastic wrap. Put in the fridge for 1 hour. Remove from the fridge and roll out into a rough circle, big enough for your pan, on a floured surface. Put into your pie pan and set aside.

2 Preheat oven to 350°F.

3 For the filling, mix all of the ingredients except for the pecans in a bowl, making sure everything is combined but not overmixed.

4 Fill the pie crust with pecans and pour the filling mixture over it until it reaches the very top (you may not use all of it). Place whole pecans on top of the pie in a neat pattern. Bake for 45 minutes (cover the edges with foil if they begin to brown before it is done) or until it has set up completely. Set aside to cool completely before cutting.

*Mini pies (as seen on the right) are a fun way to switch up how pies are served. Remember to keep an eye on them though, because they will cook a little bit faster.

My great-grandma Gussie grew up in Wrens, Georgia, in the 1920s. Her home place had both a peach orchard and a pecan orchard. They made pecan pies every week and it was the responsibility of the kids to crack and pick the nuts for the pies. Originally pecan pies were custard based. Syrup-based pecan pies became popular in the 1930s.

MINI APPLE PIES

TIME: 1 HOUR 30 MINUTES
(PLUS TIME FOR CHILLING)
MAKES: FOUR 4" MINI PIES

CRUST

- 2⅔ cups all-purpose flour
- 2 tbsp powdered sugar
- ½ tsp salt
- 1 cup cold unsalted butter, cubed
- 2 egg yolks
- 4 to 6 tbsp ice cold water

FILLING

- 8 apples
- 1 tbsp lemon juice
- ½ cup granulated sugar
- ½ cup brown sugar
- ½ tsp ground cinnamon
- ½ tsp ground nutmeg
- ¼ tsp ground allspice
- 2 tbsp all-purpose flour

1 For the crust, in a stand mixer using the paddle attachment or with a hand mixer, combine flour, powdered sugar, salt, and butter until there are only small clumps of butter. In a separate bowl, combine egg yolks and 4 tbsp of water. Change to the dough hook attachment. Pour the egg mixture into the flour mixture and mix on medium speed. Add another 1 tbsp of water if the dough is too dry. Once a dough forms, divide in half, wrap in plastic wrap, and put in the fridge for 30 minutes. Remove from the fridge and roll out one dough ball on a floured surface. Place rolled-out dough into 4 mini pie pans or one 9" pie pan, reserving second dough ball for the top crust.

2 Preheat oven to 350°F.

3 For the filling, peel and core your apples and cut them evenly into small pieces. A mandoline is useful for making even slices, but it's not required. Put in a large bowl and pour in the lemon juice. In a separate bowl, mix together sugars, spices, and flour. Pour the sugar mixture over the apples. Mix well.

4 Fill your pie crust with the apples, place rolled-out dough on top, and crimp the edges with a fork. Cut a small hole into the top for steam to escape. Brush the top of the pie with a beaten egg and bake on a rack in the middle of the oven for 45 mins to 1 hour or until golden brown. If the edges are browning too fast, cover them loosely with foil and finish baking. Take out of the oven and let cool completely.

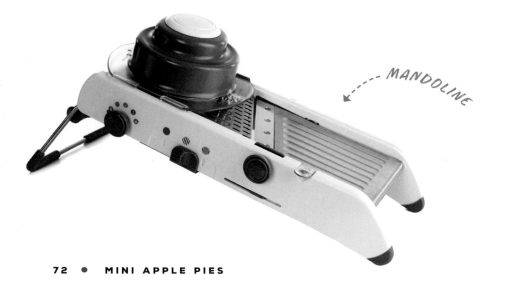

MANDOLINE

Sometimes called turnover, hand pies are just that— mini pies that fit into your hand. You can also use other delicious fruits and fillings for hand pies, such as berries, peaches, cherries, jams, and more!

APPLE HAND PIES

TIME: 1 HOUR 30 MINUTES
MAKES: 8 TO 12 HAND PIES

DOUGH

- 2 cups flour
- 1 tsp baking soda
- ½ tsp salt
- 1 tsp sugar
- ½ cup lard
- 2 tbsp very cold water

FILLING

- 3 tbsp butter
- 6 peeled, cored, and sliced
- ¾ cup brown sugar
- 1 tbsp ground cinnamon
- 1 tsp ground nutmeg
- 1 tsp ground allspice
- ½ cup chopped pecans
- 2 tbsp all-purpose flour
  Oil for frying (enough for about 3" of oil in a deep pan such as a Dutch oven)

1 For the dough, in a bowl, sift together flour, baking soda, salt, and granulated sugar. Using a fork, cut the lard into the dry ingredients. Pour in the water. Mix until the dough just comes together. Add more water if you need to, being sure not to overwork the dough. Wrap in plastic wrap and refridgerate.

2 For the filling, melt the butter in a large pan over medium-low heat until it starts to foam. Add apples and cook until they start to become soft (depending on how thick or thin you slice them, this apples, could take about 20 minutes). Add the brown sugar, ground cinnamon, ground nutmeg, ground allspice, and pecans. Add the all-purpose all-purpose flour to thicken and stir until there are no clumps of flour. Let the filling cool.

3 To assemble, roll out the dough until it's about ¼" thick. Using a large biscuit or cookie cutter (at least 5" wide), cut as many circles as you can. Add some of the filling to one side of each dough circle, dip your finger in water, and dampen the edge so it will seal. fold the other side over the filling, and press around the edges with a fork to make sure they don't open while frying. Pour the oil into a deep pan to a depth of 3" and bring the oil to 350°F (use a kitchen thermometer for this, or try the method described on page 108). Fry the hand pies in batches for about 2 minutes on each side or until golden brown. Place on a cooling rack. Enjoy warm!

APPLE CORER

CORING APPLES

The easiest way to core an apple is with an apple corer. If you don't have one, use a knife to slice the apple in half vertically. Cut each half in two again vertically. Set each apple piece on the cutting board and slice the core off. There are also ways to do it with a knife without cutting the apple into four pieces, but this is an easy way to do it if you don't need to keep your apples in one piece.

PUMPKIN PIE

TIME: 2 HOURS 15 MINUTES
MAKES: ONE 9" PIE

CRUST

- 1⅓ cups all-purpose flour
- ½ tsp salt
- 7 tbsp cold unsalted butter, cubed
- 1 egg yolk
- 2 tbsp water

FILLING

- 2 small baking pumpkins, made into puree (see the box below)
- ½ cup sweetened condensed milk
- ¼ cup maple syrup
- ¼ cup brown sugar
- 2 eggs
- 2 egg yolks
- 2 tsp ground cinnamon
- 1 tsp ground nutmeg
- 1 tsp ground allspice

1 Preheat oven to 400°F.

2 For the crust, in a stand mixer using the paddle attachment or with a hand mixer, combine flour, salt, and butter until there are only small clumps of butter. In a separate bowl, combine egg yolk and water. Pour the egg mixture into the flour mixture and mix on medium speed until a dough forms. Wrap in plastic wrap and put in the fridge for 30 minutes. Remove from the fridge and roll out into a rough circle, big enough for your pie pan, on a floured surface. Put into your pie pan, trim the excess dough, and use the tines of a fork to crimp the edges.

3 For the filling, see the information on this page to make a pumpkin puree. Lower the oven to 375°F.

4 Mix 2 cups of the pumpkin puree with the rest of the ingredients until you have a smooth custard.

5 Pour the custard into the pie crust and bake for 1 hour or until completely set up. Cover the edges with foil if they start to brown too quickly. Remove from the oven and let cool completely. Cut and enjoy!

PUMPKIN PUREE

Cut tops and bottoms off baking pumpkins. Cut each in half. Scrape out seeds. Place cut side down on a foil-lined baking sheet. Bake at 400°F for 40 minutes or until a fork pokes with no resistance. Cool. Peel skin. Puree.

BLUEBERRY PIE

TIME: 1 HOUR 30 MINUTES
(PLUS TIME TO CHILL THE DOUGH)
MAKES: ONE 9" PIE

CLASSIC CRUST
(YIELDS 2 CRUSTS)

2⅔ cups all-purpose flour
2 tbsp powdered sugar
1 tsp salt
14 tbsp cold unsalted butter, cubed
2 egg yolks
4 tbsp water

FILLING

4 cups blueberries
1 cup granulated sugar
1 tbsp lemon juice
1 tbsp cornstarch

1 For the crust, in a stand mixer using the paddle attachment or with a hand mixer, combine flour, salt, and butter until there are only small clumps of butter. In a separate bowl, combine egg yolk and water. Pour the egg mixture into the flour mixture and mix on medium speed until a dough forms. Wrap in plastic wrap and put in the fridge for 30 minutes. Remove from fridge. Roll half of it out into a rough circle on a floured surface, about ¼" thick and big enough for your pie pan. Line your pan and dock (poke holes) in the bottom of the crust with a fork. Bake at 350° for 10 minutes. Once done, set on a cooling rack to cool.

2 Preheat oven to 350°F. Bake crust for 10 minutes. Set on a cooling rack to cool.

3 For the filling, cook the blueberries in a pan over medium heat until they start to release their juice (5 to 10 minutes). Using a masher, mash them just to make sure there are no whole blueberries. Add the granulated sugar, lemon juice, and cornstarch. Cook until the mixture starts to thicken. Remove from heat. Let cool in a bowl until you're ready to use it.

4 Fill pie shell with the blueberry mixture. Use the remaining dough to place a lattice on top. Bake until the crust is golden brown, about 50 minutes. Remove from the oven and let cool.

Chocolate
PEANUT BUTTER PIE

**TIME: 1 HOUR 30 MINUTES
(PLUS TIME FOR CHILLING)
MAKES: ONE 9" PIE***

GRAHAM CRACKER CRUST

- 1 cup graham cracker crumbs
- 5 tbsp butter, melted
- ¼ cup granulated sugar
- ½ cup finely chopped salted peanuts

FILLING

- ¼ cup cornstarch
- 1½ cups granulated sugar
- ¼ tsp salt
- 3 cups milk
- 5 egg yolks
- 1 cup semisweet chocolate chips
- 2 tbsp butter

WHIPPED CREAM

- 1 cup heavy cream
- ½ cup powdered sugar
- ½ cup peanut butter

GARNISH

Semisweet chocolate chips

1 Preheat oven to 350°F.

2 For the crust, pour all of the ingredients into a bowl and stir until it forms a wet sand-like texture making, sure there are no dry patches or wet and soggy patches. Pour and press into a pie pan, making sure it's even all the way around. Bake for 10 minutes or until it has slightly browned. Set aside to cool until you're ready to use it.

3 For the filling, in a medium pot, whisk together cornstarch, granulated sugar, and salt. Add milk and egg yolks. Place over medium heat, and whisk until the mixture starts to thicken. Once it thickens to a pudding consistency and starts slightly bubbling, remove it from the heat. Add chocolate chips and butter and stir to combine.

4 For the whipped cream, put the bowl of a stand mixer and a whisk attachment into the freezer for about 10 minutes. Remove from the freezer and pour the heavy cream into the bowl. Whip on medium speed. Slowly add powdered sugar. Once all is added, turn the speed up to high, add the peanut butter, and whip until you have stiff peaks.

5 Pour the filling into the crust and put in the fridge for 4 hours. Remove from the fridge, top with the whipped cream and chocolate chips, and enjoy!

*This recipe yields one 9" pie or four 4" mini pies (like the mini pies shown at right). Mini pies bake a little faster, so keep an eye on them.

CHOPPED PEANUTS

You can buy chopped nuts for this crust, or chop them yourself using a foodprocessor. Finely chopped nuts work well, but you might try them chopped a bit more coarse, to see how you like a little more crunch!

Peanut butter and chocolate are a flavor combination that always works.

MAKING JAM

Test your jam's consistency by putting a drop onto a small ceramic plate that has been in the freezer. Next, swipe your finger through the drop. If the swipe stays and the jam doesn't come back together, it's ready.

JAM TARTS

1 HOUR 30 MINUTES
MAKES: 8 TO 12 TARTS

CRUST
- 1⅓ cups all-purpose flour
- ½ tsp salt
- 7 tbsp cold unsalted butter, cubed
- 1 egg yolk
- 2 tbsp water

FILLING
- 2 pounds berries of your choice
- ½ cup sugar
- Zest and juice of 1 lemon

GARNISH
- Fresh fruit

My mother, grandmother, and great-aunts preserve summer fruits by canning. We enjoy them year-round and even make presents of them. This recipe works well with store-bought jam for the filling, but if you have time, use the filling here, or consider making a few jars of jam and using some for tarts. These are delicious and great for a beginning baker.

1 Preheat oven to 350°F.

2 For the crust, in a stand mixer with a paddle attachment, or using a hand mixer, combine flour, salt, and butter until there are only small clumps of butter. In a separate bowl, combine egg yolk and water. Change to the dough hook. Pour the egg mixture into the flour mixture, and mix on medium speed until a dough forms. Wrap in plastic wrap. Put in the fridge for 30 minutes. Remove from the fridge and roll out on a floured surface to about ¼" thick. Cut 8 to 12 rounds 4½" to 5" in diameter (as a guide, you can use something like a cottage-cheese lid that's about the same size). Put rounds into mini tart pans. Dock (poke holes) in the bottom of each tart shell with a fork and bake for 10 minutes or until golden brown. Remove from the oven and let cool. Remove the tart shells from the pan(s) before filling.

3 For the filling, in a pot, add berries. Cook over medium heat until they become soft and start to release their juice. Mash with a potato masher just until they are no longer holding their shape. Add sugar, lemon zest, and lemon juice. Cook over lower heat if the mixture seems on the drier side and higher heat if your fruit has a lot of juice. Stir consistently until your mixture has reduced and thickened to a jam consistency. Let cool.

4 To assemble, scoop the filling out and into each tart shell, garnish with fresh fruit, and enjoy!

HOMEMADE JAM IS WORTH THE EFFORT!

FRUIT & CUSTARD TART

TIME: 1 HOUR 30 MINUTES
(PLUS TIME FOR CHILLING)
MAKES: ONE 9" TART

CRUST

½ cup + 1 tbsp unsalted butter, at room temperature

½ cup sugar

¼ tsp salt

1 egg

1¾ cups all-purpose flour

PASTRY CREAM

2 cups milk

1½ tsp vanilla bean paste or 2 tsp vanilla extract

⅔ cup sugar

6 egg yolks

¼ cup cornstarch

FRUIT

½ cup strawberries

½ cup blackberries

½ cup blueberries

¼ cup sugar

2 tbsp orange zest

½ tsp ground nutmeg

GARNISH

Powdered sugar, for dusting

1 For the crust, in a stand mixer with the paddle attachment or with a hand mixer, combine butter, sugar, and salt. Mix on medium speed until combined. Add the egg and mix. Add flour and mix until you have a dough. Wrap in plastic wrap and put in the fridge for 2 hours or overnight.

2 Preheat oven to 350°F. Roll out the dough into a rough circle on a lightly floured surface. Line a 9" tart pan with the dough. Trim and crimp the edges. Dock (poke holes) all over the bottom of the crust with a fork. Bake for 10 minutes. Once done, set on a cooling rack to cool.

3 For the pastry cream, heat milk and vanilla in a medium pot until steamy but not boiling or simmering. In a separate bowl, whisk sugar and egg yolks vigorously until the mix lightens in color and becomes airy. Add cornstarch and mix until it's completely combined. Using a ladle, spoon some of the hot milk into the egg mixture while whisking, being sure not to cook the eggs. Pour the egg mixture into the pot and heat until it thickens. Pour into a bowl and wrap in plastic wrap, making sure the plastic is touching the top of the pastry cream to prevent a skin from forming. Put in the fridge and let cool for 1 hour.

4 For the fruit, chop all of the fruit into half pieces. In a large bowl, mix fruit, sugar, orange zest, and nutmeg. Set aside.

5 To assemble, fill your tart shell to the very top with pastry cream. Strain the extra juice from the fruit and place on top. Dust with powdered sugar. Cut, serve, and enjoy.

VANILLA BEAN

FORMS OF VANILLA

Vanilla comes in beans, paste, and the dark brown extract most of us already have in our kitchens. You can use paste or extract for this recipe, but vanilla bean paste is a simple way to get a bit more potent flavor.

POP TARTS

TIME: 1 HOUR 30 MINUTES
MAKES: 9 TARTS

CRUST

1⅓ cups all-purpose flour
½ tsp salt
7 tbsp cold unsalted butter, cubed
1 egg yolk
2 tbsp water
1 egg, beaten, for egg wash

FRUIT FILLING

4 cups pitted cherries, blackberries, strawberries, or raspberries
½ cup granulated sugar
¼ cup cornstarch
Zest and juice of 1 orange

CINNAMON FILLING

½ cup brown sugar
4 tsp ground cinnamon
2 tsp all-purpose flour
½ tsp ground nutmeg
½ tsp ground allspice
1 egg

CHOCOLATE FILLING

½ cup heavy cream
1 cup semisweet chocolate chips
3 tbsp unsweetened cocoa powder
4 tbsp butter

GLAZE

1 cup powdered sugar
¼ cup milk

GARNISH (OPTIONAL)

Candy sprinkles

1 For the crust, in a stand mixer using the paddle attachment or with a hand mixer, combine flour, salt, and butter until there are only small clumps of butter. In a separate bowl, combine egg yolk and water. Pour the egg mix into the flour mixture and mix on medium speed until a dough forms. Wrap in plastic wrap and put in the fridge for 30 minutes. Remove from the fridge and roll out into a rough rectangle on a floured surface. Fold the dough over itself and turn. Fold and turn 4 times. Store in the fridge until you're ready to use it.

2 For the fruit filling, add berries to a pot and cook over medium heat for about 5 minutes, until they start to become soft and release their juice. Mash with a potato masher just until they are no longer holding their shape. Add granulated sugar, cornstarch, zest, and juice. Cook while whisking for about 2 minutes or until the mixture thickens.

3 For the cinnamon filling, whisk all the ingredients together in a bowl until there are no dry or wet patches.

4 For the chocolate filling, heat heavy cream in a saucepan over medium heat or in a microwave until just hot (not boiling). Place chocolate chips, cocoa powder, and butter in a bowl and pour hot cream on top. Whisk until smooth. Set in the fridge to cool.

5 Preheat oven to 350°F.

6 To assemble, roll out one-third of the dough until it's about ⅛" thick and trim so you have a 9" x 12" rectangle. Make two small scores every 3" on each edge of the 9" sides of the rolled-out dough. Using a sharp knife or pizza cutter, cut all the way across from score to score so that you have 3 long pieces. Do the same with the other two thirds of the dough for 9 long pieces. Brush egg wash on the dough and put about 1 tbsp of filling on one side of the dough, leaving a ½" border on the sides. Fold the other side of the dough over and press, making sure there are no air pockets. Seal the edges using a fork. Place on a parchment-lined baking sheet, brush egg wash on top, and bake for 15 minutes or until golden brown. Let them cool on a wire rack.

7 To make the glaze, mix together powdered sugar and milk in a small bowl. Decorate with candy sprinkles if desired.

EGG WASH

An egg wash is brushed over dough before baking to give it a nice golden color and shine when baked. In this recipe, the egg wash is simply a beaten egg, but sometimes the egg is mixed with water or milk.

OREO CAKE! ----->

Cakes

Cakes are one of the most fundamental desserts to know how to make. If you pay close attention while making them, you can learn a lot of important techniques and skills, like how to layer and ice, make fillings with the proper consistency, decorate, and more. The first dessert that I remember making was a chocolate cake. I made it from a box mix with my grandmother, but it started my huge interest in baking. Over the years I've made many more cakes, even a wedding cake, and I still go back to making cakes to test new flavors.

VANILLA CAKE WITH CHOCOLATE ICING

TIME: 1 HOUR 30 MINUTES
MAKES: 8 TO 12 SERVINGS,
DEPENDING ON HOW YOU SLICE IT

CAKE

- 3 cups all-purpose flour
- 1½ tbsp baking powder
- ¾ tsp salt
- 1 cup salted butter, at room temperature
- 2 cups sugar
- 4 eggs
- 1 cup milk
- 1 tsp vanilla extract

ICING

- 2 cups heavy cream
- 4 cups semisweet chocolate chips

1 Preheat oven to 350°F.

2 For the cake, in a bowl, sift together flour, baking powder, and salt. Set aside. In a stand mixer or with a hand mixer, cream the butter until fluffy. Add sugar. Continue to cream for another 8 minutes. Add eggs one at a time, making sure they're completely but not overly mixed. Add one-third of the flour mixture until combined. Combine the milk and vanilla in a cup. Add half of the milk (½ cup) and mix. Alternate the flour mixture and milk, beginning and ending with flour mixture, being careful not to overmix the batter.

3 Prepare two 6" cake pans by greasing the bases and sides, then line each base with a parchment round. Divide the batter between the pans, filling them three-quarters full. Bake for 30 minutes or until a toothpick inserted in the middle comes out clean. Set cakes aside to cool for 1 hour. Once cooled completely, run a butter knife along the edges of the cakes to release from the pan, then invert onto a cake board or plate. Using a serrated knife, cut the dome part of each cake off and cut the rest of the cake into 3 equal layers. Store in the fridge until ready to assemble.

4 For the icing, heat the heavy cream in a small pot over medium heat until it starts to lightly simmer. Put the chocolate chips in a medium-size metal bowl. Pour the hot cream over the chocolate chips and whisk until completely combined. Pour into a high-sided baking sheet or sheet cake pan and put in the fridge to cool until it has a pudding consistency. Once it is cooled, scoop the chocolate ganache out of the pan and into a stand mixer or use a hand mixer. Using a whisk attachment, whip on medium speed until it is a lighter color and has grown in size.

5 To assemble, transfer one of the cake layers onto a cake board or plate. Using an offset spatula, spread about ½ cup of the whipped ganache onto the layer. Top with the second layer and repeat until you have your desired number of layers. Using the rest of the whipped ganache, frost the top and sides of the cake.

LEVELING YOUR CAKE LAYERS

First, cool the cake completely, which makes it less likely to crack or tear. With a long serrated knife, position the blade horizontally on the side right where the cake's dome begins to rise up. With a careful sawing motion, cut about 1" into it. Rotate about 45° and repeat, working around the edge until there's a loose flap around the entire cake. Then simply saw through the middle and remove the dome. To get 4 layers out of 2 cakes, repeat this process evenly through the middle of each cake. (I often bake 2 cakes that I cut into 4 layers, but I only use 3 for the cake, so there is a leftover layer of cake that I use to crumble on top for garnish, or simply eat it!).

Before they owned their farm, my great-grandparents were sharecroppers, which meant they would give a part of each crop as rent. My mother told my brother and me a lot of stories about them and their connection to their community. They didn't have what some would consider a lot by today's standards, but they went out of their way to help others. This cake is one that my mother says was a favorite of my great-grandmother and would always come to the table when there were special visitors or holidays. I added layers, but traditionally this is a one-layer cake.

Pineapple Upside-Down
LAYERED CAKE

TIME: 1 HOUR 30 MINUTES
MAKES: 8 TO 12 SERVINGS,
DEPENDING ON HOW YOU SLICE IT

CAKE

- 3 cups all-purpose flour
- 1½ tbsp baking powder
- ¾ tsp salt
- 1 cup salted butter, at room temperature
- 2 cups granulated sugar
- 4 eggs
- 1 cup milk
- 1 tsp vanilla extract
- ¼ cup brown sugar
- 4 tbsp butter, melted, plus more for greasing cake pans
- 3 canned pineapple rings
- 9 maraschino cherries
  Melted butter for greasing cake pans

FILLING

- 1 cup chopped pineapple
- 1 cup chopped maraschino cherries

ICING

- 8 ounces cold cream cheese
- 1⅓ cups powdered sugar
- 2 cups cold heavy cream

1 Preheat oven to 350°F.

2 For the cake, in a bowl, sift together flour, baking powder, and salt. Set aside. With a stand mixer or using a hand mixer, cream butter until fluffy. Add granulated sugar. Continue to cream for 8 minutes. Add eggs one at a time, making sure they are completely but not overly mixed. Mix in one-third of the flour mixture until combined. Combine the milk and vanilla in a small cup. Add half of the milk (½ cup) and mix. Alternate the flour mixture and the milk, beginning and ending with flour mixture, being careful not to overmix the batter.

3 Prepare two 6" cake pans by greasing the bases and sides with melted butter, then line each base with a parchment round. In one of the pans, put a layer of the brown sugar and melted butter, then arrange the pineapple rings and maraschino cherries in the pan as shown. Divide the batter between the pans, filling them three-quarters full. Bake for 30 minutes or until a toothpick inserted in the middle comes out clean. Set cakes aside to cool for 1 hour. Once cooled completely, run a butter knife along the edges of the cakes to release from the pans, then invert onto a cake board or plate. Using a serrated knife, cut the dome part of the cakes off and cut the rest of the cakes so you have 3 equal layers (two plain, one decorated with the pineapple and cherries). Store in the fridge until ready to assemble.

4 For the filling, mix chopped pineapple and cherries in a bowl and store in the fridge until ready to use.

5 For the icing, use the whisk attachment of the mixer to whip the cream cheese on medium speed until smooth. Add powdered sugar and mix. Pour in cold heavy cream, and whisk on high speed until stiff peaks are achieved and icing holds lines.

6 To assemble, transfer one of the plain cake layers onto a cake board or plate. Using an offset spatula, spread about ½ cup of the icing onto the layer. Then pipe a ring of icing around the edge of the layer, and put an even layer of the chopped pineapple and cherry filling on the inside of the ring of icing. Top with the second plain cake layer and repeat until you have your desired number of layers. Top with the final decorated cake for the top. With any leftover layers of cake, use them as crumble to garnish another dessert, or simply eat it!

CARAMEL CAKE

TIME: 1 HOUR 30 MINUTES
MAKES: 8 TO 12 SERVINGS,
DEPENDING ON HOW YOU SLICE IT

CAKE
- 3 cups all-purpose flour
- 1½ tbsp baking powder
- ¾ tsp salt
- 1 cup butter, at room temperature
- 2 cups granulated sugar
- 4 eggs
- 1 cup milk
- 1 tsp vanilla extract
  Melted butter for greasing cake pans

CARAMEL
- 2 cups granulated sugar
- ½ cup heavy cream
- 6 tbsp butter
- 1 tsp salt

ICING
- 8 ounces cold cream cheese
- 1⅓ cups powdered sugar
- 2 cups cold heavy cream

GARNISH
  Caramel chips

1 Preheat oven to 350°F.

2 For the cake, in a bowl, sift together flour, baking powder, and salt. Set aside. With a stand mixer or hand mixer, cream butter until fluffy. Add granulated sugar. Continue to cream until light and fluffy, at least 8 minutes. Add eggs one at a time, making sure they're incorporated but not overly mixed. Add one-third of the flour mix until combined. In a small cup, combine milk and vanilla. Add half of the milk and mix until just incorporated. Alternate the flour mixture and milk, beginning and ending with flour mix, being careful not to overmix the batter.

3 Grease bases and sides of two 6" cake pans with melted butter. Line each base with a parchment round. Divide batter between the pans, filling them three-quarters full Bake for 30 minutes or until a toothpick inserted into the middle comes out clean. Set cakes aside to completely cool for 1 hour. Run a butter knife along the edges of the cakes to release from the pans and then invert onto a cake board or plate. Using a serrated knife, cut the dome parts of the cakes off and cut the rest of the cake into 3 equal layers (any leftover cake may be used for garnish). Store in the fridge until ready to assemble.

4 For the caramel, cook granulated sugar in a saucepan over very low heat, stirring frequently, until it melts and turns light brown. Be sure not to burn it, because it browns quickly. Once brown and 340°F to 350°F on a candy thermometer, remove from heat. Add cream while stirring. Be very careful, because it will start to bubble violently. Once it stops bubbling, add butter and salt, stirring until it is completely combined. Set aside and allow to cool before doing anything with it.

5 For the icing, in a bowl, use a whisk attachment on medium speed to whip cream cheese until smooth. Add powdered sugar. Mix until incorporated. Scrape down the sides of the bowl, pour in cold heavy cream, and whisk on high speed until stiff peaks are achieved and icing holds lines.

6 To assemble, transfer one of the cake layers onto a cake board or plate. Using a spatula, spread about ½ cup icing onto the layer. Drizzle a layer of caramel. Top with the second cake layer and repeat until you have your desired number of layers. Use the rest of the icing to frost the top and sides of the cake. Drizzle the top of the cake with caramel, and if you like, top with leftover cake crumbs and caramel chips! With any leftover layers of cake, use them as crumble to garnish another dessert or simply eat it!

Caramel cake is a classic Deep South treat that is rich and moist, with a depth of flavor.

GANACHE TOPPING

You can garnish this with chocolate ganache: 1 cup of hot heavy cream poured over 1 cup of semisweet chocolate chips and whisked until combined.

OREO CAKE

TIME: 1 HOUR 30 MINUTES
MAKES: 8 TO 12 SERVINGS,
DEPENDING ON HOW YOU SLICE IT.

CAKE
- 2 cups granulated sugar
- 1¾ cups all-purpose flour
- 1 cup unsweetened cocoa powder
- 1½ tsp baking powder
- 1½ tsp baking soda
- 1 tsp salt
- 2 eggs
- 1 cup milk
- ½ cup vegetable oil
- 2 tsp vanilla extract
- 1 cup boiling water
  Melted salted butter for greasing cake pans
- 6 Oreo cookies

ICING
- 10 Oreo cookies (cream removed)
- 8 ounces cold cream cheese
- 1⅓ cups powdered sugar
- 2 cups cold heavy cream

ASSEMBLY
- 12 Oreo cookies + extra for topping
- 1 to 2 cups milk

> **I love Oreos! This cake is fun to make and if you love Oreos like I do, you'll love this!**

1 Preheat oven to 350°F.

2 For the cake, in a bowl, sift together granulated sugar, flour, cocoa powder, baking powder, baking soda, and salt. Set aside. In a separate bowl, whisk eggs, milk, oil, and vanilla. Pour the wet ingredients in with the dry ingredients and whisk until completely combined. Add the water and whisk until completely combined.

3 Grease base and sides of two 6" cake pans with melted butter, and line each with a parchment round. Set three Oreo cookies into each of the cake pans. Divide the batter between them, filling the pans three-fourths full. Bake for 30 minutes or until a toothpick inserted in the middle comes out clean. Set cakes aside to cool for 1 hour. Once cooled completely, run a butter knife along the edges of each cake to release from the pan and then invert onto a cake board or plate. Using a serrated knife, cut the dome part of the cakes off and cut each cake into 2 equal layers. Store in the fridge until ready to assemble.

4 For the icing, first scrape the cream off of the cookies and pulse the cookies in a food processor until they are crumbs. Using a mixer with a whisk attachment, whip the cream cheese on medium speed until smooth. Add powdered sugar and mix. Scrape down the sides of the bowl, pour in cold heavy cream, and whisk on high speed until stiff peaks are achieved and icing holds lines. While whisking on low speed slowly add in the Oreo crumbs until completely mixed in, but be careful or your icing will turn from white to gray.

5 To assemble, put 9 Oreo cookies into a pan tall enough to cover them with milk. Transfer one of the cake layers onto a cake board or plate. Using an offset spatula, spread about ½ cup of the icing onto the layer and put 3 milk-soaked Oreo cookies on top of the icing, pressing them down a little bit so that the next cake layer doesn't slide. Top with the second layer and repeat until all of your layers are used. Use the rest of the icing to frost the top of the cake, then either leave the sides as shown here, or frost the sides of the cake. Crumble the remaining 3 Oreos. Decorate the top of the cake with crumbled cookies.

CHOCOLATE CHOCOLATE CAKE

TIME: 1 HOUR 30 MINUTES
MAKE: 8 TO 12 SERVINGS,
DEPENDING ON HOW YOU SLICE IT

CAKE

- 2 cups sugar
- 1¾ cups all-purpose flour
- 1 cup unsweetened cocoa powder
- 1½ tsp baking powder
- 1½ tsp baking soda
- 1 tsp salt
- 2 eggs
- 1 cup milk
- ½ cup vegetable oil
- 2 tsp vanilla extract
- 1 cup boiling water
  Melted salted butter for greasing cake pans

ICING

- 2 cups heavy cream
- 4 cups semisweet chocolate chips

1 Preheat oven to 350°F.

2 For the cake, in a bowl, sift together sugar, flour, cocoa powder, baking powder, baking soda, and salt. Set aside. In a separate bowl, whisk together eggs, milk, oil, and vanilla. Pour the wet ingredients in with the dry ingredients and whisk until completely combined. Add the water and whisk until completely combined.

3 Grease the base and sides of two 6" cake pans with melted butter. Line with parchment rounds. Divide batter between them, filling the pans three-fourths full. Bake for 30 minutes or until a toothpick inserted in the middle comes out clean. Set cakes aside to cool for 1 hour. Once cooled completely, run a butter knife along the edges of each cake to release from the pan, then invert onto a cake board or plate. Using a serrated knife, cut the dome part of the cakes off and cut each cake into 2 equal layers. Store in the fridge until ready to assemble.

4 For the icing, heat the heavy cream in a small pot over medium heatuntil it starts to lightly simmer. In a medium-size metal bowl, add the chocolate chips. Pour the hot cream over the chocolate chips and whisk until completely combined. Pour into a high-sided baking sheet or sheet cake pan, and put in the fridge to cool until it is a pudding consistency. Once it is cooled, scrape the chocolate ganache out of the pan and into a stand mixer or use a hand mixer. Using a whisk attachment, whip on medium speed until it's lighter in color and has grown in size.

5 To assemble, transfer one of the cake layers onto a cake board or plate. Using an offset spatula, spread about ½ cup of the whipped ganache onto the layer. Top with the second layer and repeat until all of your layers are used. Using the rest of the whipped ganache, frost the top and sides of the cake, or leave the sides unfrosted, as seen here. Top with leftover cake crumbs.

There is an ongoing debate in my family about when cake is chocolate cake: chocolate cake + chocolate icing or yellow cake + chocolate icing. What does your family call chocolate cake?

Coconut cake is a favorite in my family, especially with my grandpa Johnson!

COCONUT CAKE

TIME: 1 HOUR 45 MINUTES
MAKES: 8 TO 12 SERVINGS,
DEPENDING ON HOW YOU SLICE IT

CAKE

- 3 cups all-purpose flour
- 1½ tbsp baking powder
- ¾ tsp salt
- 1 cup butter, at room temperature
- 2 cups sugar
- 4 eggs
- 1 cup coconut milk
- 1 tsp vanilla extract
  Melted butter for greasing cake pans

FILLING

- ⅔ cup sugar
- 1 cup sour cream
- ¼ cup coconut milk
- ½ cup sweetened coconut flakes

ICING

- ⅓ cup water
  Pinch of salt
- ¼ tsp cream of tartar
- 1½ cups sugar
- 2 egg whites
- 2 tsp vanilla extract

GARNISH

  Coconut flakes, for topping

1 Preheat oven to 350°F.

2 For the cake, in a bowl, sift together flour, baking powder, and salt. Set aside. In a stand mixer or using a hand mixer, cream butter until fluffy. Add sugar. Continue to cream for 8 minutes. Add eggs one at a time, making sure they're combined but not overly mixed. Mix in one-third of the flour mix until combined. Combine coconut milk and vanilla in a cup. Add half of coconut milk (½ cup) and mix. Alternate flour mixture and milk, beginning and ending with flour, being careful not to overmix the batter.

3 Grease the base and sides of two 6" cake pans with melted butter. Line with parchment rounds. Divide batter between them, filling the pans three-fourths full. Bake for 30 minutes or until a toothpick inserted in the middle comes out clean. Set cakes aside to cool for 1 hour. Once cooled completely, run a butter knife along the edges of each cake to release them from the pans and then invert onto a cake board or plate. Using a serrated knife, cut the domes of the cakes off and cut each cake into 3 equal layers. Store in the fridge until ready to assemble.

4 For the filling, mix all of the ingredients together and store in the fridge until ready.

5 For the icing, set up a double boiler by placing a heatproof bowl over a pot of rapidly boiling water, making sure the boiling water does not touch the bottom of the bowl. While waiting for the water to boil, remove the bowl from the top of the double boiler, add all ingredients except vanilla to the bowl, and beat for 1 minute. Once the water is boiling, place the bowl on top. Beat constantly on high speed with the hand mixer for 7 minutes. Remove the bowl and gently fold in the vanilla.

6 To assemble, transfer one of the cake layers onto a cake board or plate. Poke holes all over the top of the cake with the handle of a wooden spoon. Pour some of the filling onto the top of the cake, just enough to cover the holes. Repeat with each layer until the filling is all gone. Cover the whole outside of the cake with the icing, and then immediately cover with coconut flakes.

Tip: Cake and filling can be done a day ahead. Just wrap with plastic wrap and refridgerate.

POUND CAKE

TIME: 1 HOUR 30 MINUTES
MAKES: 8 TO 12 SERVINGS,
DEPENDING ON HOW YOU SLICE IT

- 1 pound butter, at room temperature
- 2 cups granulated sugar
- 6 eggs
- 2½ tsp vanilla extract, divided
- 6 tbsp milk
- 2 cups all-purpose flour
- ½ cup powdered sugar
- 3 tbsp heavy cream
  Melted butter and flour for greasing the pan

ICING (OPTIONAL)
- 1 cup powdered sugar
- 3 tbsp heavy cream

1 Preheat oven to 350°F.

2 Add softened butter to the bowl of a stand mixer or use a hand mixer. Using the whisk attachment, whip until smooth. Add granulated sugar and whip until smooth and fluffy, at least 8 minutes, then add one egg at a time while whipping. Once smooth, add 2 tsp of the vanilla, milk, flour, and powdered sugar. Using the paddle attachment on low speed, mix until completely combined. Add heavy cream and remaining ½ tsp vanilla and mix until just combined. Be careful not to overmix.

3 Brush melted butter on the inside of a Bundt pan, then coat with flour. Pour the batter into the pan. Bake on the middle rack of the oven for 40 minutes or until a knife inserted in the middle comes out clean. Invert onto a plate. Cool completely.

4 For the optional icing, in a bowl, mix powdered sugar and cream together. Add more cream if too thick. When the cake is cool, drizzle the icing over the top.

ONE STICK IS ¼ POUND, SO YOU'LL NEED 4 STICKS!

STRAWBERRY SHORTCAKE

TIME: 1 HOUR 30 MINUTES
MAKES: 8 TO 12 SERVINGS,
DEPENDING ON HOW YOU SLICE IT

CAKE

- 3 cups all-purpose flour
- 1½ tbsp baking powder
- ¾ tsp salt
- 1 cup salted butter, at room temperature
- 2 cups granulated sugar
- 4 eggs
- 1 cup milk
- 1 tsp vanilla extract

FILLING

- 4 cups chopped strawberries
- 1 cup granulated sugar

ICING

- 2 cups cold heavy cream
- 1⅓ cups powdered sugar
- 2 tsp vanilla extract

1 Preheat oven to 350°F.

2 For the cake, in a bowl, sift together flour, baking powder, and salt. Set aside. In a stand mixer or with a hand mixer, cream butter until fluffy. Add granulated sugar. Continue to cream for 8 minutes. Add eggs one at a time, making sure they're combined but not overly mixed. Mix in one-third of the flour mixture. Combine the milk and vanilla in a small cup. Add half of the milk (½ cup) and mix. Alternate flour mixture and milk, beginning and ending with flour, being careful not to overmix the batter.

3 Grease the base and sides of two 6" cake pans with melted butter, and line their bottoms with parchment rounds. Divide batter between them, filling the pans three-fourths full. Bake for 30 minutes or until a toothpick inserted in the middle comes out clean. Set cakes aside to cool for 1 hour. Once cooled completely, run a butter knife along the edges of the cakes to release from the pans and then invert onto a cake board or plate. Using a serrated knife, cut the dome part of the cake off and cut each cake into 3 equal layers. Store in the fridge until ready to assemble.

4 For the filling, mix the strawberries and granulated sugar in a big bowl.

5 For the icing, using the whisk attachment of a stand mixer or a hand mixer, whip the heavy cream until it starts to slightly thicken, then slowly add the powdered sugar. Once all of the sugar is added, turn up the speed to high and whip until you have stiff peaks. Fold in vanilla.

6 To assemble, transfer one of the cake layers onto a cake board or plate. Using an offset spatula, spread about ½ cup of the whipped cream icing onto the layer. Pipe a ring of whipped cream around the edge of the layer. Put an even layer of the strawberry filling on the inside of the ring of icing. Top with the second layer and repeat until all of your layers are used. Top with the rest of your whipped cream and strawberries.

CINNAMON ROLLS! ---->

4

Snacks & Breads

This chapter has a mix of quick and easy recipes as well as some more involved ones, but all are worth it. These miscellaneous treats are a great way to move out of your baking comfort zone and test your knowledge. There are things from yeasted dough like beignets and cinnamon rolls, to sticky buns, scones, and granola.

IS YOUR COOKING OIL THE RIGHT TEMPERATURE FOR FRYING?

A kitchen thermometer can tell you if your oil is the right temperature. Without a thermometer, one easy way that's a bit safer than some others is to stick the end of a wooden spoon into the oil. If bubbles form around the wood and start to float up, your oil is ready. If it's bubbling hard, the oil is too hot, so turn the heat down, let it cool a bit, and check it again (have an adult help you).

BEIGNETS

TIME: 2 HOURS 30 MINUTES
MAKES: 12 BEIGNETS

DOUGH

- 3¾ cups bread flour
- 1 tsp salt
- 3 tbsp granulated sugar, divided
- 1 cup warm milk (between 96°F and 100°F)
- 2 tsp active dry yeast
- 1 egg
- 3 tbsp unsalted butter, melted
- Oil for frying (enough for about 3" of oil in a deep pan such as a Dutch oven)

GARNISH

- Powdered sugar

> In 2017, I got to go to New Orleans to be on *Kids Baking Championship* on Food Network! While I was there, I ate my way through the city. One of my favorite things was beignets! They are a type of French yeasted fried dough, and they are delicious, especially served hot! Since this recipe involves frying with hot oil, be sure to have an adult help you, especially if it's your first time trying this.

1 For the dough, in a stand mixer fitted with the paddle attachment or with a hand mixer, combine flour, salt, and 2 tbsp of the granulated sugar. In a separate cup, combine milk, yeast, and the remaining 1 tbsp of granulated sugar. Let it sit until it becomes foamy. On low speed, add the egg to the dry ingredients, then slowly pour in the yeast mixture until a shaggy dough forms. Switch to the dough hook attachment and knead on medium-low speed while slowly adding the butter. Turn the speed up to medium, and knead for about 5 minutes or until a sticky dough forms but you can still handle it. Place in a separate greased bowl and cover with plastic wrap. Let it rise for 2 hours.

2 For frying, once the dough has risen, turn it out onto a floured table or countertop. Using a rolling pin, roll it out into a rough rectangle about 6" x 8". Cut into 12 rectangles. Pour oil into a deep pan to a depth of 3" and bring to 325°F. Fry in batches for about 1 minute on each side or until golden brown. Remove from oil and put on a cooling rack (you will want to set this on a cookie sheet or some other surface to catch the oil).

3 Dust with a generous amount of powdered sugar and enjoy hot!

COOKING THERMOMETER

CINNAMON ROLLS

TIME: 3 HOURS
MAKES: 9 ROLLS

TANGZHONG

(See page 114)

1½ tbsp granulated sugar
 1 tbsp all-purpose flour
1½ tbsp milk
1½ tbsp water

DOUGH

2½ tsp instant dry yeast
 ½ cup + 2 ½ tbsp lukewarm
    milk (96°F to 100°F)
 3 cups bread flour
 ¾ tsp salt
 3 tbsp granulated sugar
2½ tbsp water
 2 eggs, at room temperature
 1 egg yolk, at room
    temperature
 4 tbsp unsalted butter, at
    room temperature
    Cooking spray

FILLING

¼ cup brown sugar
¼ cup toasted sugar
   (toasting sugar is optional;
   see box)
 2 tbsp ground cinnamon
 1 tsp ground nutmeg
 1 tsp ground allspice
 5 tbsp butter, melted or
    browned (see page 115)

GLAZE

1½ cups powdered sugar
 ⅛ tsp salt
 ¼ cup heavy cream
 ½ tsp vanilla extract

1 For the tangzhong, in a small pot, whisk together all the ingredients. Place over medium heat, and cook until it becomes a thick paste. Set aside to cool.

2 For the dough, combine yeast and milk in a small bowl. Set aside until it becomes slightly foamy on top. Add flour, salt, and granulated sugar to a stand mixer bowl or use a hand mixer. With the dough hook attachment, stir on medium-low speed. While stirring, add the yeast/milk mix, water, tangzhong, eggs, and egg yolk. Knead on medium-low speed to form a smooth dough. Add butter 1 tbsp at a time, completely combining before adding the next 1 tbsp. When butter's mixed in, knead for 5 minutes. Remove from the bowl. Spray the bowl with oil or cooking spray. Return the dough to the bowl, cover with a damp towel, and let rise in a warm place for 1½ hours.

3 For the filling, whisk together all the dry ingredients.

4 To assemble, roll dough into a rectangle about ½" thick. Brush on melted butter, making sure it's not too hot. Evenly sprinkle on filling mix. Tightly roll the dough into a log, cut off the ends to make them even, then cut into 9 equal pieces. Place in a greased baking pan (3 rows of 3). Let rise at room temperature for 1 hour.

5 Preheat oven to 350°F.

6 Bake at 350°F for 30 minutes. Cool slightly, then ice.

7 For the glaze, whisk together powdered sugar and salt. Whisk in cream slowly until desired consistency is reached. Whisk in vanilla. Cover the rolls with glaze and enjoy!

TOASTED SUGAR

Toasting sugar changes the flavor profile in an interesting way, adding a kind of nutty hint to it. It's made by pouring an entire bag of sugar onto a large baking sheet and putting it in a 300° F oven for 1 hour, then removing it from the oven and whisking thoroughly. Bake for another 4 hours whisking, every 30 minutes. Store like regular sugar.

WHY SOUR CREAM?

Sour cream donuts are great because they don't have to rise, once cooked the outside has cracks that hold onto the glaze, and they have a great texture.

Sour Cream
DONUTS

TIME: 1 HOUR 30 MINUTES
MAKES: 8 TO 12 DONUTS

DONUTS

- 3 cups bread flour
- 2 tsp baking powder
- 2 tsp salt
- 2 tbsp unsalted butter, at room temperature
- ½ cup granulated sugar
- 4 egg yolks
- 1 egg
- ½ cup sour cream
  Oil for frying (enough for about 3" oil in a deep pan such as a Dutch oven)

GLAZE

- 4 to 5 cups powdered sugar
- ⅛ tsp salt
- ¼ cup pure maple syrup
- 1 tsp vanilla extract
- ¾ cup boiling water

1 For the donut dough, sift flour, baking soda, and salt together in a bowl. In a stand mixer fitted with the paddle attachment or with a hand mixer, combine butter, granulated sugar, and egg yolks. Add half of the flour mixture to the butter/sugar/egg mixture, and mix until well combined. Add the sour cream. Mix until well combined. Add the rest of the flour. Mix until well combined. Put in a bowl and cover with plastic wrap. Place in the fridge for an hour. Once cooled and rested, dump out onto a floured countertop and roll out the dough until it is about ½" thick. Using a round biscuit cutter or donut cutter, cut out as many doughnuts as possible. Reroll if needed.

2 Pour the oil to a depth of about 3" in a deep pan and heat to about 350°F (you can use a kitchen thermometer for this, or try the method described on page 108), and fry in batches for about 2 minutes on each side or until golden brown. Remove from the oil and put onto a cooling rack.

3 For the glaze, in a bowl, combine the powdered sugar and salt. Whisk to remove any lumps. Add maple syrup and vanilla. Slowly whisk in boiling water. Whisk until completely smooth and at your desired consistency.

4 To assemble, completely submerge each donut in the glaze and let the excess drip off on a cooling rack. Let the glaze dry completely, and enjoy!

DONUT CUTTER ----->

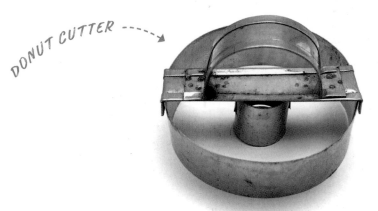

STICKY BUNS

TIME: 1 HOUR 45 MINUTES
MAKES: 8 TO 12 BUNS

TANGZHONG
1½ tbsp toasted sugar (see page 110)
1 tbsp all-purpose flour
1½ tbsp milk
1½ tbsp water

DOUGH
2½ tsp instant dry yeast
½ cup + 2½ tbsp lukewarm milk
3 cups bread flour
¾ tsp salt
3 tbsp toasted sugar (see page 110)
2½ tbsp water
2 eggs, at room temperature
1 egg yolk, at room temperature
4 tbsp unsalted butter, at room temperature
Oil for greasing bowl

GLAZE
½ cup unsalted butter or browned butter (see page 115)
¼ cup brown sugar
¼ cup toasted sugar (see page 110)
3 tbsp molasses
1½ cups toasted pecans

FILLING
¼ cup brown sugar
¼ cup toasted sugar
2 tbsp ground cinnamon
1 tsp ground nutmeg
1 tsp ground allspice
5 tbsp butter, melted or browned (see page 115)

1 For the tangzhong, in a small pot, whisk together all the ingredients. Turn the heat to medium and cook until it becomes a thick paste. Set aside to cool.

2 For the dough, in a cup, pour the yeast into the milk and set aside until it becomes slightly foamy on top. In a stand mixer bowl or with a hand mixer, add flour, salt, and toasted sugar. Using the dough hook attachment, stir on medium-low speed. While stirring, add the yeast milk mixture, water, tangzhong, eggs, and egg yolk. Knead at medium-low speed until it's one cohesive dough. Once smooth, add butter 1 tbsp at a time, making sure the butter is completely combined before adding the next tbsp. Once all the butter is mixed in, knead for 5 minutes. Remove from the stand mixer bowl and spray the bowl with oil. Put the dough back in the bowl. Cover with a damp towel and let rise in a warm place for 1½ hours.

3 For the glaze, in a small pot, add the all the ingredients, except the pecans. Over medium heat, stir until the butter's melted and everything is combined. Pour into a greased tall-sided square baking sheet or baking dish, about 9" x 9". Pour the pecans over it and set aside until you're ready to use it.

4 For the filling, in a bowl, whisk together all of your dry ingredients and set aside.

5 To assemble, roll out the dough into a rectangle about ½" thick. Brush on all of your melted butter, making sure it's not too hot or else you will kill the yeast. Evenly sprinkle over your filling mixture. Tightly roll up the dough into a log. Cut off the ends of your log just to make it even. Cut the log into 9 equal pieces. Place into the pan with the glaze in 3 rows of 3. Let rise at room temperature for 1 hour.

6 Preheat oven to 350°F.

7 Bake at 350°F for 30 minutes. Set aside to cool down slightly. Once cooled, run a butter knife along the edge, invert onto a cooling rack, and enjoy!

TANGZHONG

Tangzhong is a yeast bread technique with Asian origins that makes breads soft and less crumbly. It involves cooking some flour and liquid before adding the remaining ingredients.

BROWNED BUTTER

Browned butter is made by melting butter completely in a saucepan over medium-high heat, continuously stirring until it foams up and browns (when you see dark brown specks on the bottom of the pan). If it starts foaming a lot, remove it from the heat until it calms down, then put it back to finish. Cool by pouring it into a baking sheet or dish and freezing it.

Crème brûlée is easier to make than it may seem. Plus it's a great way to learn how to make custard.

Coffee CRÈME BRÛLÉE

TIME: 1 HOUR 30 MINUTES
MAKES: 8 SERVINGS

- 2 cups heavy cream
- ½ cup coffee beans
- 1 tsp instant coffee
- 6 egg yolks
- ¾ cup sugar, plus more for topping
- Pinch of salt

1 Preheat oven to 350°F.

2 Combine the heavy cream and coffee beans in a pot. Steep the coffee beans over medium for 10 minutes, being sure not to allow the cream to boil. Strain the coffee beans out of the cream, stir in instant coffee, and keep cream hot. In a separate bowl, whisk the egg yolks and sugar together until they become lighter in color and slightly foamy. Pour about ½ cup of the hot cream into the egg mixture, pour it all back into the pot, and stir to combine. Pour into eight 6" ramekins and place on a tall-sided baking sheet. Pour boiling water into the baking sheet and bake for 30 minutes or until barely set up. Set in the fridge for 4 hours or up to overnight.

3 Top each custard with a thin layer of sugar, and broil about 4" from the heat until golden brown, 4 to 6 minutes. Enjoy!

Cinnamon Apple Nut
MUFFINS

TIME: 1 HOUR 30 MINUTES
MAKES: 8 TO 12 MUFFINS

MUFFINS

6 tbsp salted butter, at room temperature
2 cups brown sugar
2 eggs
1 egg yolk
1 cup applesauce
⅓ cup sour cream
1 cup all-purpose flour
½ cup rolled oats
¾ tsp baking soda
½ tsp salt
2 tsp ground cinnamon
½ cup chopped pecans
½ cup diced apples

CRUMBLE

¾ cup rolled oats
¾ cup almond flour
½ cup brown sugar
1½ tsp ground cinnamon
½ tsp salt
½ cup chopped pecans
6 tbsp butter, melted

1 Preheat oven to 350°F.

2 For the muffins, using a stand mixer fitted with the paddle attachment or with a hand mixer, cream butter and brown sugar together until fluffy. Add eggs and egg yolk. Combine completely. Add applesauce and mix until smooth. Add sour cream and mix until fully combined. In a separate bowl, combine all of your dry ingredients except for the apples. Pour your dry ingredients into the wet ingredients and mix until smooth. Fold in the apples.

3 For the crumble, combine everything in a bowl except for the butter. Slowly pour in the butter while stirring until you have a crumbly consistency.

4 To assemble, fill large cupcake tins with liners. Using an ice cream scoop, fill each liner three-fourths of the way. Cover the entire tops with some of the crumble and bake for 25 minutes or until a toothpick inserted into the middle of a muffin comes out clean.

BAKING APPLES

For most baking, you want apples that stay somewhat crisp, such as Granny Smith, Honeycrisp, or Braeburn. You don't want apples that turn to mush when baked.

PECAN GRANOLA

TIME: 25 MINUTES
MAKES: 8 TO 12 SERVINGS

4 cups whole oats
  (not instant)
½ cup chopped pecans
1 cup salted butter,
  melted
1 cup brown sugar
4 tbsp ground cinnamon
1 tsp kosher salt
1 tsp maple extract

1 Preheat oven to 350°F.

2 In a big bowl, mix the oats and pecans. Pour butter over the oats and add brown sugar. Mix thoroughly. Add cinnamon, salt, and maple extract. Make sure there are no dry spots or wet spots.

3 Pour granola onto a baking sheet lined with parchment paper and bake for about 20 minutes, stirring about every 5 minutes. Set aside to cool completely and enjoy on yogurt or as a snack by itself!

OTHER GRANOLA INGREDIENTS

Now that you know the basics of making homemade granola, you can try other ingredients, such as different kinds of nuts, dried fruit, coconut, seeds, and other spices to find your own combinations!

SCONES

TIME: 1 HOUR 30 MINUTES
MAKES: 12 SCONES

5   cups all-purpose flour
1   tbsp baking powder
½   tsp baking soda
¾   cup sugar, divided
1   tsp salt
1   cup very cold salted butter, cubed
1½ cups buttermilk
1   cup frozen blueberries, strawberries, peaches, blackberries, or raspberries
3   tbsp salted butter, melted
½   cup canned fruit such as peaches

1 Preheat oven to 400°F.

2 In a stand mixer fitted with a paddle attachment or with a hand mixer, mix flour, baking powder, baking soda, ½ cup of the sugar, and salt. Add cold butter. Mix until there are only pea-size pieces of butter left. Add buttermilk. Mix on low speed until the dough comes together. Fold in the fruit. Turn the dough out onto a floured surface and form into a rough rectangle about 1" thick. Cut into 12 rectangles or triangles. Brush with butter, melted and sprinkle with remaining ¼ cup of sugar. Bake for 20 minutes. Remove from the oven and eat warm with jelly or butter.

ABOUT SCONES

Scones are a great way to work with different seasonal fruits. You can eat scones for breakfast or as a snack and they can be sweet or savory (these are a sweet version). They're great with jelly or butter and some tea or coffee!

GINGERBREAD

TIME: ABOUT 1 HOUR
MAKES: 8 TO 12 SERVINGS

- ½ cup salted butter
- ½ cup sugar
- 1 egg
- 1 cup molasses (unsulfured)
- ½ cup unsweetened applesauce
- 2½ cups all-purpose flour
- 1½ tsp baking soda
- 2 tsp ground cinnamon
- 2 tsp ground ginger
- 1 tsp ground cloves
- ½ tsp salt
- 1 cup hot water

1 Preheat oven to 350°F.

2 In a stand mixer with the whisk attachment or with a hand mixer, mix butter and sugar on medium speed until well combined and smooth. Add the egg and whisk until incorporated. Add molasses and applesauce.

3 Combine flour, baking soda, spices, and salt in a bowl. Add this to the molasses mixture and whisk in the hot water until combined. Pour batter into a greased 8" square cake pan. Bake for about an hour or until a toothpick inserted in the center comes out clean.

CLOVES

CINNAMON

GINGER

INDEX

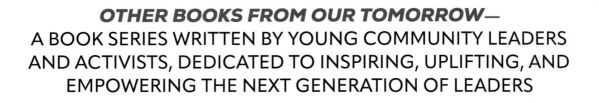

OUR TOMORROW

OTHER BOOKS FROM OUR TOMORROW—
A BOOK SERIES WRITTEN BY YOUNG COMMUNITY LEADERS AND ACTIVISTS, DEDICATED TO INSPIRING, UPLIFTING, AND EMPOWERING THE NEXT GENERATION OF LEADERS

Books N Bros: 44 Inspiring Books for Black Boys (Sidney Keys III)

From teen entrepreneur and literacy advocate Sidney Keys III, a reading guide that centers on Black boys, inspired by the success of his book club Books N Bros. Featured books include *Hidden Figures: Young Readers' Edition* by Margot Lee Shetterly, *Black Boy White School* by Brian F. Walker, and *Shuri: A Black Panther Novel* by Nic Stone.

ISBN 9781684620487

Kindness Is My Hobby: How to Change the World Right Where You Are (Ruby Kate Chitsey)

Ruby Kate Chitsey, the teenage founder and CEO of Three Wishes for Ruby's Residents, shares how she spreads kindness every day and how you can do it too, with activities inspired by her own initiatives that have gained her national attention. Projects include Senior Pen Pal Project, Mobile Book Cart, and Postcards of Kindness.

ISBN 9781684620609